SpringerBriefs in Computer Science

For further volumes:
http://www.springer.com/series/10028

David B. Skillicorn

Understanding
High-Dimensional Spaces

 Springer

David B. Skillicorn
School of Computing
Queen's University
Kingston, ON
Canada

ISSN 2191-5768   ISSN 2191-5776   (electronic)
ISBN 978-3-642-33397-2   ISBN 978-3-642-33398-9   (eBook)
DOI 10.1007/978-3-642-33398-9
Springer Heidelberg New York Dordrecht London

Library of Congress Control Number: 2012948185

ACM Computing Classification (1998): H.2, E.1, I.2

Printed on acid-free paper

Springer is part of Springer Science+Business Media (www.springer.com)

Preface

High-dimensional spaces arise naturally as a way of modelling datasets with many attributes. Such a dataset can be directly represented in a space spanned by the attributes, with each record of the dataset represented as a point in the space with its position depending on its attribute values. Such spaces are not easy to work with because of their high dimensionality: our intuition about space is not reliable, and measures such as distance do not provide as clear information as we might expect.

High-dimensional spaces have not received as much attention as their applications deserve, partly for these reasons. Some areas where there has been substantial research are: images and video, with high-dimensional representations based on one attribute per pixel; and spaces with highly non-convex clusters. For images and video, the high dimensionality is an artifact of a direct representation, but the inherent dimensionality is usually much lower, and easily discoverable. Spaces with a few highly non-convex clusters do occur, but are not typical of the kind of datasets that arise in practice.

There are at least three main areas where complex high dimensionality and large datasets arise naturally. The first is data collected by online retailers (e.g. Amazon), preference sites (e.g. Pandora), social media sites (e.g. Facebook), and the customer relationship data of all large businesses. In these applications, the amount of data available about any individual is large but also sparse. For example, a site like Pandora has preference information for every song that a user has listened to, but this is still a tiny fraction of all of the songs that the site cares about. A site like Amazon has information about which items any customer has bought, but this is a small fraction of what is available.

The second is data derived from text (and speech). The word usage in a set of documents produces data about the frequency with which each word is used. As in the first case, all of the words used in a given document are visible, but there are always many words that are not used at all in it. So such datasets are large (because easy to construct), wide (because languages contain many words), and sparse (because any document uses a small fraction of the possible words).

The third is data collected for a security, defence, law enforcement or intelligence purpose; or collected about computer networks for cybersecurity. Such datasets are large and wide because of the need to enable as good solutions as possible by throwing the data collection net wide. This third domain differs from the previous two because of greater emphasis on the anomalous or outlying parts of the data rather than the more central and common place.

High-dimensional datasets are usually analyzed in two ways: by finding the set of clusters they contain; or by looking for the outliers—almost two sides of the same coin. However, these simple strategies conceal subtleties that are often ignored. A cluster cannot really be understood without seeing its relationships to other clusters "around" it; and outliers cannot be understood without understanding both the clusters that they are nearest to, and what other outliers are "around" them. The development of the idea of local outliers has helped with this latter issue, but is still weak because a local outlier is defined only with respect to its nearest non-outlying cluster.

In this book we introduce two ideas that are not completely new, but which have not received as much attention as they should have, and for which the research results are partial and scattered. In essence, we suggest a new way of thinking about how to understand high-dimensional spaces using two models: the *skeleton* which relates the clusters to one another, and *boundaries in empty space* which provides a new perspective on outliers, and on outlying regions.

This book should be useful to those who are analyzing high-dimensional spaces using existing tools, and who feel that they are not getting as much out of the data as they could; also their managers who are trying to understand the path forward in terms of what is possible, and how they might get there. The book assumes either that the reader has a reasonable grasp of mainstream data mining tools and techniques, or does not need to get into the weeds of the technology but needs a sense of the landscape. The book may also be useful for graduate students and other researchers who are looking for open problems, or new ways to think about and apply older techniques.

Acknowledgments

My greatest debt is to Mike Bourassa. Discussions in the course of his doctoral research first surfaced many of the ideas described here, and we had many long conversations about what it meant to be interesting, before we converged on the meaning that is expanded here. I am also grateful to all my students who, by providing an audience for me to explain both simple and complex ideas, help me to understand them better.

Kingston, April 2012   David Skillicorn

Contents

1 Introduction 1
  1.1 A Natural Representation of Data Similarity 3
  1.2 Goals 8
  1.3 Outline 10

2 Basic Structure of High-Dimensional Spaces 13
  2.1 Comparing Attributes 13
  2.2 Comparing Records 14
  2.3 Similarity 14
  2.4 High-Dimensional Spaces 16
  2.5 Summary 18

3 Algorithms 19
  3.1 Improving the Natural Geometry 19
     3.1.1 Projection 20
     3.1.2 Singular Value Decompositions 20
     3.1.3 Random Projections 22
  3.2 Algorithms that Find Standalone Clusters 23
     3.2.1 Clusters Based on Density 23
     3.2.2 Parallel Coordinates 24
     3.2.3 Independent Component Analysis 24
     3.2.4 Latent Dirichlet Allocation 25
  3.3 Algorithms that Find Clusters and Their Relationships 25
     3.3.1 Clusters Based on Distance 25
     3.3.2 Clusters Based on Distribution 26
     3.3.3 Semidiscrete Decomposition 27
     3.3.4 Hierarchical Clustering 29
     3.3.5 Minimum Spanning Tree with Collapsing 29
  3.4 Overall Process for Constructing a Skeleton 30

3.5   Algorithms that Wrap Clusters   31
       3.5.1   Distance-Based   32
       3.5.2   Distribution-Based   32
       3.5.3   1-Class Support Vector Machines   32
       3.5.4   Autoassociative Neural Networks   33
       3.5.5   Covers   34
3.6   Algorithms to Place Boundaries Between Clusters   34
       3.6.1   Support Vector Machines   35
       3.6.2   Random Forests   35
3.7   Overall Process for Constructing Empty Space   36
3.8   Summary   37

4   **Spaces with a Single Center**   39
4.1   Using Distance   39
4.2   Using Density   40
4.3   Understanding the Skeleton   42
4.4   Understanding Empty Space   43
4.5   Summary   45

5   **Spaces with Multiple Centers**   47
5.1   What is a Cluster?   48
5.2   Identifying Clusters   50
       5.2.1   Clusters Known Already   50
5.3   Finding Clusters   50
5.4   Finding the Skeleton   55
5.5   Empty Space   58
       5.5.1   An Outer Boundary and Novel Data   58
       5.5.2   Interesting Data   60
       5.5.3   One-Cluster Boundaries   63
       5.5.4   One-Cluster-Against-the-Rest Boundaries   63
5.6   Summary   64

6   **Representation by Graphs**   67
6.1   Building a Graph from Records   68
6.2   Local Similarities   68
6.3   Embedding Choices   69
6.4   Using the Embedding for Clustering   70
6.5   Summary   71

7   **Using Models of High-Dimensional Spaces**   73
7.1   Understanding Clusters   73
7.2   Structure in the Set of Clusters   76
       7.2.1   Semantic Stratified Sampling   77
7.3   Ranking Using the Skeleton   78

7.4 Ranking Using Empty Space.   87
     7.4.1 Applications to Streaming Data   89
     7.4.2 Concealment.   90
7.5 Summary   91

8 Including Contextual Information.   93
8.1 What is Context?.   93
     8.1.1 Changing Data   93
     8.1.2 Changing Analyst and Organizational Properties.   94
     8.1.3 Changing Algorithmic Properties   95
8.2 Letting Context Change the Models.   95
     8.2.1 Recomputing the View   95
     8.2.2 Recomputing Derived Structures.   96
     8.2.3 Recomputing the Clustering   97
8.3 Summary   98

9 Conclusions   99

References   103

Index   107

Chapter 1
Introduction

Many organizations collect large amounts of data: businesses about their customers, governments about their citizens and visitors, scientists about physical systems, and economists about financial systems. Collecting such data is the easy part; extracting useful knowledge from it is often much harder.

Consider, for example, the tax collection branches of governments. Most governments create a record for each resident and business each year, describing their incomes, their outflows that can be used as deductions, their investments, and usually some demographic information as well. From this information they calculate the amount of tax that each resident and business should pay.

But what else could they learn from all of this data? It is a very large amount of data: there is one record per citizen and business (a tax return); and each record contains a large number of pieces of information, although of course most of these values are null or zero for most returns.

One kind of knowledge that governments spend a lot of effort to acquire is whether, who, and by how much individuals and businesses are providing false information that results in them owing (apparently) less tax. A strategy for detecting this is to compare people or businesses of the same general kind, and see whether there are some that seem qualitatively different, without any obvious explanation of why. In other words, one way to discover tax fraud is by exploiting *similarity* among the income and outflows of individuals, expecting that similarity of record values should be associated with similarity of tax payable.

This strategy works quite well and is routinely used by tax departments, targeting one year dentists, say, and another year flight attendants. Of course, this means that tax cheats in other professions receive less scrutiny (until their turn comes up). It would be attractive for governments to do this kind of assessment globally (for all taxpayers) every year, but there are several problems: pragmatically, the size of the data makes the necessary computations alarmingly large; but, more significantly, we do not yet understand clearly how to represent and analyze the structure of the space implicit in such a collection of data. If a particular taxpayer looks unusual within the set of taxpayers of the same general kind, is it because they are paying less tax

D. B. Skillicorn, *Understanding High-Dimensional Spaces*, SpringerBriefs
in Computer Science, DOI: 10.1007/978-3-642-33398-9_1, © The Author 2012

than they should be, or is it because of some other difference between them and the set to which they are being compared. Does it matter which set they are compared to—other dentists, or all other taxpayers? In other words, there are deep issues to do with the concept of "similarity", and these issues are complicated by the size and richness of the datasets that we would like to analyze.

The focus of this book is on ways to think about structure and meaning associated with such large, complex datasets; algorithms that can help to understand them; and further analyses that can be applied, once a dataset has been modelled, that provide payoffs in many different domains (including tax fraud detection).

The data that we will consider, at least initially, is *record* data, that is data that consists of a set of records, each of which contains a number of fields that hold values. Thus the data naturally forms a table or matrix. Throughout, n will be used to denote the number of records, and so the number of rows of the table or matrix, and m will denote the number of values in each record, which are called *attributes*. Provided that each record contains the same number of values, the data forms a matrix with n rows and m columns.

The values that a field can hold are often numeric, but there is no intrinsic reason why a field cannot hold other types of information such as a piece of text. So, in the taxation example, some fields, such as income, hold numbers; while other fields, such as occupation, holds strings. (Of course, in this example, all occupations could be given numeric codes and so converted from strings to numbers but this is not always feasible.)

The kind of datasets we will consider have two properties which make their analysis difficult:

- The datasets are wide, that is they have many attributes. Often they will have many records too but, in general, it is the number of attributes that creates the conceptual difficulties.
- The number of attributes reflects the inherent complexity of the data, and so of the system being modelled, rather than arising from a particular choice of representation of the system. For example, one way to represent images is to regard them as records with one attribute for each pixel. While this can sometimes be useful, the apparent complexity of the representation does not necessarily match the real underlying complexity of the set of images. In other words, it is possible to choose representations that create apparent complexity that isn't really there.

The other critical aspect to the problems we will address is that the expected structure cannot be straightforwardly inferred from the problem domain. Returning to the taxation example, we can certainly imagine some ways in which the data might be manipulated to reduce apparent tax payable. For example, incomes might be altered to appear smaller than they are, and deductions inflated; these are quite natural properties to suspect and so to look for. A more sophisticated inspection tactic is based on Benford's Law [42] which describes the expected distribution of digits in certain kinds of real-world numbers—for example, the first digit in such a number is much more likely to be a 1 than a 9. When humans make up numbers, for example a deduction that doesn't really exist, they tend to choose the first digit much more uniformly. Knowing this, numbers in a tax return can be scored by how unusual they are with respect to Benford's Law, and undocumented, unlikely numbers are treated as suspicious.

However, there are presumably many more subtle aspects of the content of tax returns that are even more useful for detecting tax fraud. There is usually no obvious *a priori* way to look for them—and, sadly, intuition about suspicious patterns has sometimes been quite unreliable.

If we cannot find these kinds of alterations in the data and the implied structure and similarity of records by looking for them explicitly using predetermined models of the underlying mechanisms, how can we find them? What has turned out to be a powerful approach is to build models of the structure in the data *inductively*, that is letting the data reveal its own structure. Once the structure of the data is understood, subsequent questions about unusual parts of this structure become easier to answer. So *inductive data analysis* or *inductive modelling* is at the heart of the approach we will be describing.

This is not to say that there is not sometimes a role for *pattern-based* understanding of large datasets. For example, humans have been coming up with ways to manipulate financial accounts since financial accounts were invented, and so any auditor has a long list of possible frauds and the associated patterns they create in data; tax and insurance investigators do too. The credit card industry is the leading example of this; they have accumulated many examples of what people do to carry out credit-card fraud, and they turn popular examples into rules that are used to check new transactions. Nevertheless, novel forms of creative accounting continue to be discovered, so the set of patterns is always growing and never, at any moment in time, exhaustive. So the role for inductive model building and pattern discovery is to make sure that novel and unsuspected structures are noticed. In these example settings, not all of these induced structures will be suspicious—but all need to be considered as potentially suspicious until proven otherwise. A recent survey by Kriegel et al. [35] provides more background on pattern-based clustering.

1.1 A Natural Representation of Data Similarity

We now turn to the question of how to construct a measure for the similarity of each pair of records that accurately reflects intuitive ideas of similarity between the entities (people, objects, transactions) that the records describe. Such a measure should be reflexive (so that a record is similar to itself) and symmetric (so that if A is similar to B then B is also just as similar to A). It is less clear how similarity should behave transitively: if A is similar to B and B is similar to C, then how similar is A to C? Mostly a measure that obeys the triangle inequality is plausible and well-behaved, but this is not an obligatory requirement.

Any dataset has a natural geometric space in which it can be represented, the space spanned by its attributes. Each attribute defines one axis of a space, and each record is represented by a point that is placed at the position corresponding to the

Fig. 1.1 Points derived from
height and weight values of a
population

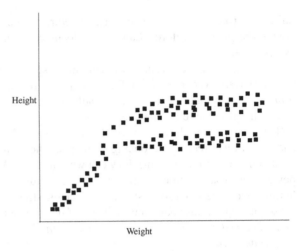

Height

Weight

values of its attributes. In other words, a row of the dataset is interpreted as a set of m
coordinates in the space. So, for a very simple dataset recording people's heights and
weights, there would be two axes, one for height and one for weight, and each person
would be represented by a point whose position is determined by the value of their
particular height and weight. This is illustrated in Fig. 1.1. In this representation, a
number of properties of human heights and weights become visible. For example,
heights and weights are reasonably well correlated; but the relationship between the
two is slightly different for men and women; and the range of heights and weights is
different for children and adults. These properties did not have to be looked for; they
emerge inductively from looking at the data in a particular way. The way in which
they are looked at matters: looking at a table of height-weight pairs makes it much
harder to see these relationships than the simple visualization in the figure.

Unfortunately, real datasets are not often so well-behaved. Some of the problems
that arise are:

- The units in which each attribute's values are expressed make a difference to the
  apparent similarity, but there is no natural or principled way to choose these units.
- The attributes are often collected for reasons unrelated to modelling, so that important ones are missed, irrelevant ones are collected, and some subsets of those
  collected may be measuring the same underlying property. This also distorts the
  apparent similarity.
- Algorithms that collect sets of unusually similar records into *clusters* often have
  to be told what clusters look like and (usually) how many clusters there are, but
  this is often little better than a guess. Hence the results may depend heavily on the
  parameter choices rather than on the data itself.
- Many clustering algorithms silently cluster together records that are not actually
  very similar, especially lumping small numbers of records in with a larger set of
  mutually similar records to which they are only modestly similar.

Fig. 1.2 Individual clusters are identical but the clustering is different

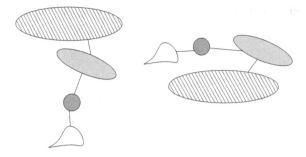

We will return to these issues in subsequent chapters.

There are two levels of understanding the structure of a dataset. The first is to understand where the data *is* and what it looks like. At its simplest, this could be just applying some clustering algorithm to the dataset, and evaluating the structure associated with the resulting clusters:

- How many clusters are there (but this often requires encoding, in the clustering algorithm, assumptions about what a cluster means and how many there should be, so can often be a bit circular)?
- What are the clusters like? Do they have characteristic sizes (the number of records they contain), shapes (in the natural geometry, for example, are they spherical, or elliptical, or more spider-like), and densities (are all members of a cluster equally similar)?

At a more sophisticated level, it might be useful to know if there are records that do not fit into any cluster in a plausible way, and how many of these unusual records there are. Concentrating on such unusual records is called *outlier detection* [2].

In general, though, a deeper understanding comes from seeing how the clusters and these few unusual records (which could be considered clusters of size one) are *related* to one another. Figure 1.2 shows two simple clusterings with the same number and size of clusters—but we would clearly consider the datasets described by each to be qualitatively different—both the connections between pairs of clusters and their position relative to one another is quite different. This global structure, that includes both the clusters *and* their relationships to each other, we will call the *skeleton* of the dataset. The skeleton includes relational information about the similarity between clusters; and the similarity between clusters need not be of the same qualitative kind as the similarity between records.

A part of understanding the skeleton is to understand what each cluster represents, that is why the records within a cluster are considered similar in some cluster-wide sense. This is a surprisingly difficult problem. A clustering algorithm or approach considers some set of the records to be similar to one another, but this does not immediately tell us what property this mutual similarity is capturing—although we can be confident that, given appropriate attributes and algorithms, it is capturing *something* real about the system that the dataset describes. Sometimes it is possible to compute

Fig. 1.3 Individual points
with different significance

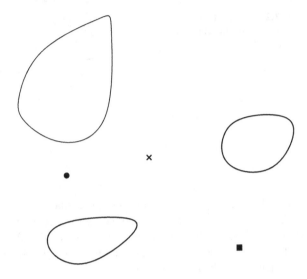

the centroid of each cluster which becomes a kind of artificial record that resembles
closely all those in the cluster. Examining the values of the attributes of this artificial
record can suggest the cluster's "meaning" but this is hit-and-miss in practice.

The neglected second level of understanding the structure of a dataset, is to consider the places where data *isn't*, that is to consider the empty space in the natural
representation. First of all, understanding the empty spaces is another way of understanding the relationships in the skeleton. For example, a record in empty space can
be of vastly different significance depending on *where* in the space it is. A simple
example is shown in Fig. 1.3. The three labelled points (cross, disk, and square) are
all far from any of the clusters—and yet we are tempted to regard them as representing records of quite different kinds. Empty space, therefore, is not uniformly bland
but rather has a structure all of its own. Some locations in this structure are more
significant than others.

If the problem is to understand the structure of a single, once-for-all dataset, then
all we need is this view of almost-empty space—it provides a way to categorize
isolated points that refines the skeleton structure induced by the clusters.

However, if the problem domain, and so dataset, is one where new data sometimes
appears, either via some uncontrolled mechanism or because it is requested, then
the structure of empty space becomes much more important and useful. A new
record that appears in a space close to or inside an existing cluster brings little
or no new information about the real-world system. A new record that appears in
empty space, however, introduces new information and its meaning depends on
where in the empty space it appears. For example, a new record might suggest that
two of the existing clusters are actually parts of a single cluster; or that there is
another previously unsuspected cluster; or that the data has a much greater extent
than previously realized. Furthermore, if new data can be explicitly requested, then

Fig. 1.4 Hierarchy of significance of isolated points, and
of the regions they are in

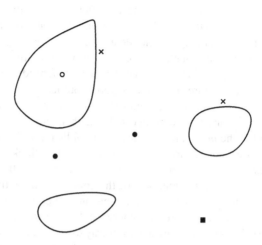

the structure of empty space suggests what kinds of new records will be most useful
to request.

This understanding of where new data records might reveal more about the structure of the dataset can be lifted to an understanding of *regions* of empty space and
their (potential) significance. We can divide such regions into five different categories, depending on what the arrival of a new record in each indicates. These five
categories are illustrated in Fig. 1.4, against a background of a few representative
clusters.

The five categories, and their meanings, are:

- *normal* records, indicated by circles. These fall within existing clusters and so
  represent "more of the same".
- *aberrant* records, indicated by crosses. These lie on the outskirts of an existing
  cluster (whatever that means for a particular clustering technique) but their position
  is readily explainable by the finiteness of the data used for clustering. They also
  represent "more of the same" (or perhaps "more of almost the same").
- *interesting* records, indicated by solid circles. These lie in empty space *between* the
  existing clusters. Their presence suggests that the current model or understanding
  of the space is inadequate.
- *novel* records, indicated by solid squares. These also lie in empty space but on the
  "outside" of the entire clustering. They do not have the same implications about
  the structure of the model because they are so different from the data from which
  the model was built. They imply that the data collection was inadequate, rather
  than that the model built from it was inadequate.
- *random* records, indicated by squares. These lie so far from other data that the
  suspicion is that something has gone wrong with the data collection rather than
  that there is previously unsuspected data.

Novel records correspond to what are often called, in the literature, *outliers*, records that do not fit into the existing clusters and that therefore need to be understood in a different way—although outlier detection often conflates novel and random records. Interesting records roughly correspond to what are often called *local outliers* [11, 48]. They also tend to be regarded as records that need to be understood in a different way, one that is more subtle than (global) outliers.

We claim that interesting points should not be regarded as outliers, but understood in a deeper way, in two respects. First, their presence implies that something is deficient in the *model*, that is they have implications for the system and not just for their own existence. Second, it is not helpful to think of them as outliers from a *particular* cluster, as is usually the case in the local outlier literature, but as outliers from the skeleton. In other words, the concept of an outlier, as such, is not helpful because it suggests records (points) that are somehow less relevant or less important, rather than records that reveal otherwise difficult-to-see structure in the data.

These five categories are a helpful way to understand the structure of empty space, as a counterpoint to the structure implied by the skeleton. Exactly how they come into play depends on the problem domain, as we shall see.

We have described them as properties of newly arriving records and how these records might be interpreted. These categories can also be understood as descriptions of certain regions of space. In other words, a region might meaningfully be considered an interesting region, or a novel region. This is useful in some situations because these regions can be used to generate requests for the collection of new data that are expected to be particulary revealing. As well as providing a way to interpret particular kinds of *answers*, these categories can also define particular kinds of *questions*.

1.2 Goals

The primary and immediate goal of the kind of analysis we have been talking about is understanding: understanding what clusters are like and what they represent, understanding the relationships among clusters; understanding which records do not really belong to any cluster (or which form a cluster of size 1); and understanding the spaces in between clusters. Such analysis reveals structure and meaning in the real-world system from which the data came.

A clustering begins with information about the pairwise similarities between (some subset of) the records. This information induces four things, each of which can be considered emergent from the pairwise local information:

1. The structure of a space in which the clustering takes place, which we will call a *statistical geometry*.
2. The clusters themselves, defined by those records that are sufficiently similar that they are collected together semantically. Clusters have properties and structure, and also have relationships with one another, relationships that are of a different qualitative kind from the relationships among records.

3. Global pairwise similarity between every pair of records, derived from the global integration of the (partial) pairwise similarities, which modifies and enriches the local similarity structure.
4. A changed view of the initial pairwise similarity between related records—it may be weaker or stronger in the global context than it was when considered purely locally.

These emergent properties are invisible at the level of each individual record, or even when considering the relationships between pairs of records. Extracting them via the global integration implicit in any clustering is therefore a powerful way of understanding a dataset.

One class of important structures that can be built on understanding of the dataset are *rankings*. The structure enables the records to be organized in new ways, the simplest of which is a linear ordering of all of the records based on some property of the skeleton.

A ranking does not necessarily require constructing a space from the dataset. The set of records could be ordered (sorted) according to the values of one particular attribute. For example, tax departments might investigate individuals starting with those with the largest income, using the rationale that discovering fraud by such people brings in the greatest amount of extra money. This idea can be extended to any function that combines the attributes; for example, a tax department might compute the sum of income and deductions for each taxpayer and use this to sort the list of taxpayers. Those at the top of the sorted list might be plausible targets for investigation because they make a lot of money; but for two people with the same income the new function ranks the one with the greater deductions higher.

The problem with constructing such a function is that it embodies a kind of pattern that has to be known in advance; someone has to decide which attributes are important, whether they are positively or negatively related to the goal property, and how they should be weighted and combined. These are not easy decisions in most settings.

The advantages of building a space and a clustering in an emergent way, and then using them as the basis for ranking is that the properties of the space emerge from the properties of the data and so do not have to be known in advance. In the simplest case, imagine the points corresponding to the records in some space and sweep a plane across the space from one side to the other, inserting each record into an ordered list as the plane encounters that record. If the orientation of the plane is chosen appropriately (a complex issue we will postpone for now) then the ordering will be derived from the data. In fact the plane describes a function on the attributes but the way in which they are combined and weighted has been inferred from the data, rather than constructed beforehand by an expert.

Another useful kind of ranking is from the "middle" of the data to the "outside" (or *vice versa*) where both "middle" and "outside" are intuitively obvious but practically rather difficult. Often the "middle" represents data that are common or "normal" while the "outside" represents data that are unusual or anomalous. So in situations where the anomalies are the records that deserve further attention (the tax example, many kinds of fraud, intrusion detection) such rankings focus attention on some of the records, those at one end of the ranking. On the other hand, if the records represent documents, the document closest to the "middle" is somehow the most representative and so might be the place to starting learning about whatever the set of documents describes.

Global rankings are useful because the records at both ends of the ranking are special in different ways, and the rankings allow us to find them and perhaps focus more attention on them.

It is sometimes the case that what is of interest is not a global ranking, but the ranking in the neighborhood of one particular record. As before, it is possible to address this without necessarily constructing a global space—in the natural space spanned by all of the attributes, find the closest neighbors of the given point (closest in the sense of, say, Euclidean distance). This has the same drawbacks as ranking without constructing a space—any metric that defines "neighbors" treats all of the attribute differences as of equal importance.

In a constructed space, there are two advantages when trying to find the neighbors of a given point. First, similarity measures take place in a space where the selection and weighting of attributes has been made globally; second, the skeleton makes it computationally easy to choose a smallish set of points that *could be* neighbors and compute similarity to them, rather than having to compute similarity to all possible neighbors and then discard those who are too far away (too dissimilar).

One thorny issue that remains is that of *context*. Everything so far has assumed that the same space will do for every purpose; but often the person doing the analysis has extra domain knowledge or knowledge about the particular dataset that should be accounted for. We have argued above that, in general, not enough is known about which attributes are most important and by how much, nor about how these choices depend on the structure in the real world. However, a particular person analyzing the data may know enough to discount a particular attribute, or to know that a particular discovered cluster represents a known problem with data collection, and it would be helpful if there were a way to include this knowledge in the construction of the space. Furthermore, it is often useful to be able to ask "what if?" questions about the data, which might require discounting or enhancing the effect of an attribute or a record.

1.3 Outline

Chapter 2 introduces the natural mapping of record-based data to high-dimensional space, introduces some of the difficulties of working in such spaces, and discusses the choices that have to be made to define pairwise similarity between points (and so the pairwise similarity between records). Chapter 3 introduces the algorithmic toolkit that we will use to understand high-dimensional spaces, including techniques for projection, knowledge discovery algorithms for many kinds of clustering, and some prediction techniques. Most of these techniques are well-known in the knowledge-discovery community, but their use is sometimes slightly specialized for this problem.

Chapter 4 introduces the two main ideas of the book: the skeleton as a way to understand the relationships among clusters, and the importance of empty space in helping with understanding—but within the setting of a single global cluster, which represents the common, but too simplistic, understanding of the problem. Chapter 5 generalizes this to the more realistic case where the data contains multiple clusters, each with its own internal properties, but related to one another in potentially complex ways. The skeleton now becomes essential to understanding these relationships. Modelling empty space also becomes much more significant because empty space is not just *around* the skeleton structure, but also *in between* the clusters.

Chapter 6 introduces a different approach for transforming record data to a geometry. Instead of embedding records as points and then using their positions in the embedding to define pairwise similarity, this chapter introduces the ideas of calculating pairwise similarity directly (creating a graph), and then embedding this graph.

Chapter 7 illustrates the many value-added analyses that can be carried out once a high-dimensional space has been modelled. These are primarily based on different kinds of *rankings* of the dataset records. Such rankings are more sophisticated, by a wide margin, than those derived directly from the raw data, because the skeleton and empty space models represent a global integration of all of the data, which provides a context or background against which to make ranking decisions.

Chapter 8 addressed the difficult issues associated with including context in the understanding. The data, the algorithms, and the background knowledge and goals of an analyst all change with time. This could be handled by rebuilding all of the models to respond to any change. It is, though, much more useful to work with more intermediate structures: so that the effects of the contextual changes can be precisely observed, and so that human understanding gained from one model can be leveraged to understand the next.

Chapter 2
Basic Structure of High-Dimensional Spaces

Data is naturally represented geometrically by associating each record with a point in the space spanned by the attributes. This idea, although simple, raises a number of challenging problems in practice.

2.1 Comparing Attributes

For any single attribute, it is not necessarily the case that the significance of the values it can take depends linearly on those values. For example, for an attribute that measures income, almost all of the values will be between 0 and a few hundred thousand (almost regardless of currency); however, there will be a few individuals whose income is three or four decimal orders of magnitude greater than this. Should this huge difference in income amount be treated as a huge difference in significance? Perhaps, but there's at least a case that it should not. One plausible way to address this would be to discretize attribute values into ranges with semantics; for example, incomes could be placed into a few categories such as *low*, *medium*, *well-off*, *wealthy*, and *super-rich*.

However, there is then the problem of how to measure differences in the values of a single attribute between two different records. The significance of a difference does not follow immediately from an understanding of the significance of a magnitude. For example, small differences may plausibly be treated as no difference at all.

The most common (dis)similarity measure based on the natural geometric embedding is *Euclidean distance*—but this measure is built from the *squares* of the differences in the values of each individual attribute. It therefore implicitly claims that, for differences, significance grows much faster (quadratically) than magnitude.

D. B. Skillicorn, *Understanding High-Dimensional Spaces*, SpringerBriefs
in Computer Science, DOI: 10.1007/978-3-642-33398-9_2, © The Author 2012

2.2 Comparing Records

When the data has more than one attribute, a new difficulty appears. To compare
two records, we must compare the differences in the values of two or more attributes
measuring different things. How can we combine the difference for each attribute
into a difference between the whole records? There is no straightforward way to do
this—it really is comparing apples and oranges. This applies even if both attributes
are measuring the quantity or number of "the same" underlying objects, for example
dollar amounts or word frequencies. Similarity depends on the range and distribution
of the values that each attribute takes over the whole dataset, not just on the kind of
objects that it describes.

The standard approach, although it is difficult to justify, is *normalization*. Normalization means converting the raw values for each attribute into a standardized form
that is the same for all attributes. For example, a common approach to normalization,
for each attribute, is to compute the mean and standard deviation of the values of that
attribute across the entire dataset. In the data table or matrix, this means computing
the mean and standard deviation of each column. The values in the column corresponding to the attribute are then converted by subtracting the column mean from
each value, and dividing the result by the column standard deviation. For the entire
set of values of each attribute, subtracting the mean centers them around zero, with
roughly half positive and half negative. Dividing by the standard deviation makes
the ranges of all of the attributes roughly comparable. If the original attribute values
were drawn from a Gaussian distribution, this normalization maps two-thirds of the
values to the range between -1 and $+1$. This normalization is called *z-scoring*.

Other normalizations are possible. For example, the values of each attribute could
be mapped into the range 0–1, but the effect depends on the maximum and minimum
values taken by the attribute more than on the distribution of values it possesses in the
dataset. Calculations of the mean could be trimmed, that is some of the largest and
smallest values could be omitted to give a more robust estimate of the distribution
of values.

2.3 Similarity

So now suppose that all of the attributes have been normalized in some reasonable
way. There are still choices about which kind of function will be used to combine
the per-attribute similarities.

By far the most common way to do this combining is to use Euclidean distance
between the points corresponding to each record. Of course, distance is a *dissimilarity* measure since points that are far apart are not similar to one another—but
the relationship between distance and similarity is straightforward and we can think
about it either way.

Viewed geometrically, using Euclidean distance seems sensible; it's the way we
think about distance in the real world. But Euclidean distance between the points

corresponds to taking the difference in the values for each attribute, *squaring it*, and then adding up these squares and taking a square root. The squaring step means that two records with a large difference in the values of only a single attribute seem disproportionately far apart because of the impact on the sum of this one term. From this perspective, Euclidean distance seems less obvious.

Other common distance calculations include: Manhattan distance (sum the differences for each attribute), or Hamming distance (sum the number of times the values for each attribute are different, regardless of how much).

There is a practical problem with computing distances or similarities as well. If n is large (there are many records) then n^2 distance calculations need to be done, and this may simply be too expensive. Fortunately, for the purpose of understanding the global structure of the data, only the other points fairly close to each point need to be looked at, and this creates the opportunity for some optimizations that we will see later. But the quadratic complexity of computing all of the pairwise distances means that some common approaches do not scale to large, high-dimensional (many attribute) datasets.

The next layer of complexity comes from the choice of attributes. For most datasets, it is not clear from the beginning which attributes will turn out to be important, so there is a natural tendency to collect any attributes that *might* be. The presence of these extra attributes makes the natural geometric space seem to be of higher dimension than it really is—and this, of course, alters the apparent similarity between each pair of records. For example, a single extra attribute with uniform random values for each entry will pull all of the records slightly further apart than they "should" be, but by a random amount, so blurring the similarity structure.

A more subtle problem happens when a subset of the attributes are measuring almost the same property but in different ways. At a macroscopic scale, this means that the values of each pair of attributes in the subset must be highly correlated. The effect of this redundant subset is that records that differ in this underlying property seem much more different than they should be, because the difference gets added into the sum multiple times.

If the set of attributes are well correlated then the solution is obvious—remove all but one of the attributes from the dataset. This tends not to work in practice—often two attributes will be strongly correlated over much of their range but uncorrelated over the rest, and it is not clear whether this latter range is important. Correlation is also not transitive, which further complicates trying to remove redundant attributes.

Finally, most real-world clusters are actually *biclusters*, that is, within each subset of the records similarity depends on only a small subset of the attributes, and this subset is different for each cluster. Ignoring this property, and computing distances using all of the attributes, blurs the tightness of each cluster and makes them all harder to detect. Datasets that contain biclusters are often analyzed with algorithms that simultaneous try to cluster the records *and* the attributes. There is an inherent symmetry in the data in this case: records are similar because of a particular subset of the attributes, but attributes are also similar because of a particular subset of the records.

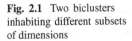

Fig. 2.1 Two biclusters inhabiting different subsets of dimensions

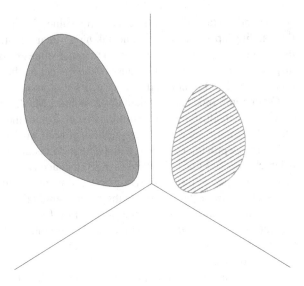

Figure 2.1 shows two biclusters and illustrates some of the difficulties. Naive analysis, perhaps based on distance, makes the bottom of both clusters seem similar so such an algorithm might discover three clusters, the top of each of the visible clusters, and a third consisting of the bottom halves of both.

2.4 High-Dimensional Spaces

Now we turn to issues that arise because of the high-dimensional nature of the natural space, issues which test our intuition developed in three-dimensional space. First of all, in high-dimensional spaces, distances do not behave quite as we expect. Let us suppose a dataset with m attributes (so an m-dimensional space) and suppose that the attribute values in each record are divided into three simple categories: large and positive, large and negative, and close to zero. Now consider records whose attribute values are equally likely to be one of these three categories. How likely is it that such a record will be close to the origin in the m-dimensional space? This can only happen if all of its attribute values are in the close-to-zero category, and the chance of this is $(1/3)^m$. This is an extremely small probability when m is large. In other words, if the records have uniformly chosen entries, almost all of them will lie far from the origin.

Now consider any two records. How likely is it that they are close to each other? This can only happen if their entries, for every attribute, match; that is, they are both large and positive, both large and negative, or both close to zero. The probability of this is, again, $(1/3)^m$ and so extremely small when m is large.

In other words, in high-dimensional spaces, uniformly randomly distributed points are all far from each other. The impact on data with more structure is that the relative distances from a point to its nearest neighbor and its furthest neighbor are similar, especially in relation to the absolute distances to both. This is why indexing schemes such as k-d trees that allow nearest neighbors to be found in low-dimensional spaces do not scale to high-dimensional spaces—they have an often-ignored exponential dependence on the dimensionality.

One approach to this problem is to view the space spanned by the attributes as a vector space instead of a Cartesian space. In this view, each point is regarded as the endpoint of a vector from the origin. Each point, therefore, has two associated properties: its *distance* from the origin, and its *direction* from the origin. These aren't new properties, just a different way of looking at the same set of points, just like converting from Cartesian to polar coordinates.

However, this new view makes it possible to see that two points (vectors) in the same direction from the origin might be considered similar even though they end at quite different distances. Two such points have the same *pattern* of attribute values but differ only in the *magnitudes* of these values, and in a proportional way. The records are alike in some deeper sense, but one has "more of the same" than the other. In some situations, this kind of similarity makes a great deal of sense. It is called *cosine similarity* because the cosine of the angle between the vectors to two points a and b is given by

$$\cos \theta = \frac{a \cdot b}{|a| \, |b|}$$

where the dot denotes the dot product of the two vectors, $a_1 \times b_1 + a_2 \times b_2 + \cdots a_m \times b_m$, and $|a|$ is the norm (length) of the vector a.

Equivalently, each row of the dataset can be divided by its length, as another form of normalization of the data. This has the effect of mapping the data points into a kind of hypersphere around the origin. The angle between two vectors is now just their dot product (since the norms are all now 1). Two vectors that point in roughly the same direction have a large dot product (close to $+1$) so the cosine of the angle between them is large and θ is close to $0°$. Two vectors that are close to orthogonal have a dot product close to zero and θ is close to $90°$. Two vectors that point in roughly opposite directions have a dot product close to -1 and θ is close to $180°$.

So cosine similarity gives a different view of similarity, and so of clustering, based on projecting the data points onto a unit hypersphere. The sphere is still high-dimensional, so the problems of working in high-dimensional space have not gone away, but this form of similarity might be more appropriate for some data.

We are interested in datasets in which m is large, but the value of n, the number of records, is also relevant. There are three cases:

- n is about the same size as m so the dataset matrix is roughly square.
- n is much bigger than m. This tends to be the common case, for in many applications it is always possible to collect more data, perhaps just by waiting a little longer. Large values of n make it difficult to compute all pairwise distances, so better

algorithms are required to elicit the relationships among points. For example, if the distance from a to b is large and c is close to b, then it follows that a is far from c and this distance does not have to be explicitly calculated.

- n is smaller than m. In this case, the data cannot occupy more than an n-dimensional subspace of the m-dimensional space; in other words, it must be the case that the data occupies a lower-dimensional manifold in the high-dimensional space. This is not directly helpful because it is not, in general, possible to know how the lower-dimensional space is oriented inside the high-dimensional one, but it does help with some of the structure-discovery algorithms we will describe later.

It is common in the literature to claim that, in this case, a substantial number of the attributes can be discarded *a priori*. Although this is sometimes the case, more often than not it is impossible to discard attributes without deeper analysis.

2.5 Summary

The mapping from dataset records to points in the space spanned by the attributes is a natural and appealing one, but it contains hidden complexities. For local similarities to be sensible after such an embedding, choices need to be made about the relative scaling of the axes (the relationship between magnitude and significance for each attribute *and* the relative magnitudes between pairs of attributes). A similarity function needs to be defined—Euclidean distance seems natural in the geometric setting, but seems less so when its meaning for record similarity is considered. And high-dimensional spaces are unintuitive, with distances behaving in unexpected ways.

All of the choices made about embedding and similarity have a large impact on the resulting models—but there is usually no principled way to make many of them, at least until the domain is well understood. Such problems are ubiquitous in knowledge discovery; the usual solution is to iterate the embedding/model-building cycle; and that is usually what is required here.

Chapter 3
Algorithms

This chapter describes many of the algorithms that play a role in constructing models of high-dimensional spaces. Those familiar with knowledge discovery may want to skip some or all of the chapter. However, several of the standard algorithms are used in slightly specialized ways when applied to high-dimensional datasets.

The algorithms fall into several groups. First, there are preliminary techniques that address the difficulties of working in high-dimensional spaces by projecting, in some way, into spaces of lower dimension. Second, there are algorithms that discover clusters in a dataset, but do so in such a way that the relationships among discovered clusters are not computed, or at least not computed in usable ways. Third, there are algorithms that both discover clusters and also the relationships among them, at least partially. These two classes of algorithms are the building blocks of the skeleton describing a dataset. Fourth, there are algorithms that "wrap" a cluster, providing it with some form of boundary that defines which points lie within the cluster and which lie outside. Fifth, there are algorithms that construct boundaries between one cluster and the rest of the data, that is predictors. These last two classes of algorithms provide ways to understand the structure of empty space around and between the skeleton.

3.1 Improving the Natural Geometry

As we pointed out in the previous chapter, high-dimensional spaces are awkward places both to work with and to understand. For many real datasets, they are also unnecessarily complex, because the underlying dimensionality of the data is smaller than it appears. Although this seems wrong-headed, it often happens in practice because the fundamental attributes of the system are not understood when the data is collected. For this reason, and because it is human nature, attributes are collected in case they are helpful, rather than because they are known or expected to be helpful.

D. B. Skillicorn, *Understanding High-Dimensional Spaces*, SpringerBriefs
in Computer Science, DOI: 10.1007/978-3-642-33398-9_3, © The Author 2012

3.1.1 Projection

An obvious improvement is to *project* the high-dimensional space into some lower-dimensional space, and carry out analysis in the lower-dimensional space.

Of course, the lower-dimensional space must be faithful to the high-dimensional one so that the structure that is discovered is the same as, or at least consistent with, the structure in the original space. So the form of the projection must be carefully chosen to ensure that this happens.

Projection into a lower-dimensional space does not necessarily have to lose structure. If the data really is a lower-dimensional manifold in the high-dimensional space then a projection can preserve its structure exactly. Even when this is not the case, a projection that removes dimensions in which the data has a small extent can lose information that can be regarded as noise, and produce a structure that is arguably better than the original.

There are two main families of algorithms for projecting a high-dimensional space in a sensible way. The first uses singular value decomposition to project based on the variation present within the data. The second uses projections that include an element of randomness, but that come with some kind of guarantee not to project in a "bad" direction.

Projections do not, in themselves, help to build the skeleton, but they pave the way for such constructions. At the same time, they often provide hints about properties of the data that can be useful in themselves, and also can guide the skeleton-building step. In particular, projections to two or three dimensions can be visualized and so reveal elements of the structure directly to a human analyst.

3.1.2 Singular Value Decompositions

Matrix decompositions transform the data matrix by expressing it in the form of a product of other matrices, in which different aspects of the dataset are visible. We will see the use of several different matrix decompositions in this chapter. Each makes some particular assumption about the kind of structure present in the data, and teases it out. These implicit structures play different roles in understanding the data.

The most useful of these matrix decompositions is Singular Value Decomposition (SVD) [20, 22, 29]. SVD corresponds to an affine transformation (a rotation and stretching) of the natural geometry of a dataset—a reorientation in which the new axes are placed along directions in which the dataset has large variation.

Suppose that the dataset is represented by an $n \times m$ matrix, A, with $n \geq m$. Then the singular value decomposition of A expresses it as the product of three other matrices like this:

$$A = U\,S\,V'$$

where the superscript dash indicates matrix transposition (swapping rows for columns), U is an $n \times m$ orthogonal matrix (so $UU' = I$), V is an $m \times m$ orthogonal matrix, and S is a diagonal matrix (its off-diagonal entries are all zeros) and its diagonal entries are non-increasing.

The interpretation of the right-hand side of this equation is: the rows of V' (so columns of V) describe new axes, with the property that the first row is the axis along which the data varies the most, the second row is the orthogonal axis along which the data varies second most, and so on. The orthogonality of the axes means that uncorrelated variation is being captured. The diagonal entries of S captures the relative magnitude of the variation along each axis. The rows of U are the coordinates of the point corresponding to each record relative to the new axes.

If the data matrix is unnormalized, say it consists only of non-negative values, then the cloud of data points lies somewhere in the positive hyperquadrant, and the direction of maximal variation is necessarily from the origin to the center of this data cloud. In other words, the first axis captures a property rather like a mean of the entire dataset. This can be useful—for example, it forms the heart of Google's PageRank [12] algorithm—but it is also limited. The orthogonality property forces the second axis to be orthogonal to the first, but this direction is not necessarily one in which the data cloud varies the most. Hence the second and subsequent rows of V' do not reveal useful properties of the data.

The SVD is much more revealing if the data matrix is normalized so that the data cloud is centered at the origin and scaled to remove "accidental" variation. Moving the data cloud to the origin is achieved by subtracting the mean value from each column. Scaling to remove accidental variation is achieved by dividing the entries in each column by the standard deviation of that column. In other words, the "correct" normalization required for SVD is z-scoring.

A particular case that often comes up is when the matrix is sparse, that is has many zero entries. The mean of a column of such a matrix has a numerator that depends on the non-zero entries but a denominator that depends on all of the entries. It therefore blurs the available information because the denominator is large relative to what it "should be". For such data, it is often more useful to normalize by computing the column mean and standard deviations of only the non-zero entries and altering only these entries as well. The zero entries remain zero after normalization. Such a normalization assumes that median values of attributes have the same meaning as zero values of attributes, which is sometimes plausible and sometimes not.

The usefulness of SVD for constructing a skeleton is twofold. First, by transforming the space it becomes possible to see structure that might have been hidden by the particular presentation of the data. For example, if the data occupies a more or less flat k-dimensional manifold in the m-dimensional space, then this is detectable because the $k + 1$st and subsequent singular values will be small. Another way to think about this is that the SVD is expressing the dataset in terms of k *latent* factors rather than the original m factors, one associated with each attribute. These k factors are expected to be more essential than the perhaps accidental attributes that were actually collected for the dataset. Even if the dataset is not quite a flat submanifold, the existence of small singular values provides some indication of how many dimensions are important.

Second, truncating the representation at any value of k creates U_k, an $n \times k$ matrix, S_k, a $k \times k$ matrix, and V'_k, a $k \times m$ matrix. The implied representation in k-dimensional transformed space is as faithful as any k-dimensional representation can be. For example, choosing $k = 2$ or 3 means that the first k columns of U can be treated as coordinates, plotted, and visualized. Furthermore, the magnitudes of the singular values after the point of truncation estimate how much of the variation is being ignored by truncating there.

In some datasets it is plausible that some of the variation observed is the result of "noise", which really means variation arising from some process that we are not interested in modelling. Provided this unmodelled process has only small effects on the dataset, this variation will appear along later axes in the decomposition and with small associated singular values. This "noise" can be ignored by truncation; we can also remultiply the three truncated matrices to produce a new matrix A_k that can be regarded as a "denoised" version of A.

SVD followed by truncation is therefore one way to "project" high-dimensional data into lower dimensions. Its advantage is that the actual dimensions into which the data are projected are derived from the structure of the data itself; in other words the projection itself has an inductive component.

3.1.3 Random Projections

SVD is just one way of projecting the data, and there could be many others, although SVD guarantees to be, in a certain sense, the best. However, it is also relatively expensive, so there has always been interest in cheaper projections that are almost as good.

There is an extensive literature on random projections, but we will show only one example. An Achlioptas matrix, R, of size $m \times k$ is defined by:

$$r_{ij} = \sqrt{s} \begin{cases} +1 \text{ with probability } \frac{1}{2s} \\ 0 \text{ with probability } 1 - \frac{1}{s} \\ -1 \text{ with probability } \frac{1}{2s} \end{cases}$$

The parameter s defines both the sparsity with which the data matrix is sampled and the sparsity of the resulting projection since about $1/s$ of the entries in R are non-zero. k is the dimensionality of the space into which the data will be projected.

A data matrix, A, can be postmultiplied by an Achlioptas matrix to produce a matrix that is $n \times k$. Each row of the resulting matrix is interpreted as the coordinates of a point in k-dimensional space resulting from the projection. Analysis of the structure of a dataset can now begin from this k-dimensional space rather than the original m-dimensional space. The Achlioptas projection comes with a guarantee about how little the Euclidean distance between each pair of points is distorted relative to their distance in the original space [1]. Depending on the precise definition of similarity, clustering in the projected space will therefore tend to reflect the clustering of the original, high-dimensional space.

Random projection techniques do not provide any information about how to choose either the number of dimensions into which to project, or about the choice of s.

3.2 Algorithms that Find Standalone Clusters

The second step of the analysis is to discover the clusters that are present in the data. There are different points of view on what constitutes a cluster. In some settings, all points must fall into some cluster so there may be clusters than only consist of single points. In other settings, a collection of similar points must meet some criterion, perhaps being of a certain size or density, to qualify as a cluster. In that case, some points (and even sets of points) may not belong to any cluster.

In this section we concentrate on algorithms that find each cluster independently so that any relationships that exist between clusters are not computed. The results of these algorithms enable us to add a cluster label to each record of the dataset, but this does not, by itself, create much understanding of what the clustering reveals about the data. Getting such understanding will require further, downstream analysis.

3.2.1 Clusters Based on Density

Density-based clustering algorithms [18] start from the assumption that a cluster is characterized by a set of points that are sufficiently mutually similar. A typical algorithm starts by choosing one of the points at random as a cluster seed; adding all of the points that are sufficiently similar to the seed into the cluster; and then repeating with more sufficiently similar points until there are no further candidates for addition. There are many refinements; for example, in the early rounds of addition there may be an additional requirement that added points have many neighbors who are also to be added. In general, there is a tension between being able to add points on "arms" that radiate from some central core, and not adding points that are too isolated from the core. There is also usually a requirement that a cluster be of a certain minimum size.

Once a cluster has been completed, its points are removed from the dataset and a new seed point selected to begin the next cluster. If a partial cluster cannot be expanded to the required minimum size, then its points are replaced in the dataset (such points could still participate in other clusters seeded from a different part of the dataset).

The entire process ends when no further clusters can be found. Records remaining in the dataset are not part of any cluster, and are categorized as isolated points.

One of the advantages of density-based clustering is that the number of clusters does not have to be specified in advance—the algorithm will continue to find new clusters as long as sufficiently dense constellations of points exist.

3.2.2 Parallel Coordinates

For datasets with a modest number of attributes, perhaps up to a hundred, parallel coordinates [26] can reveal something about the clustering using a visualization.

Each attribute is represented by a vertical line, marked with a scale derived from the range of the values taken by that attribute in the dataset. Each record is represented by a point on each of the vertical lines whose position depends on the value of that attribute in the record; and all of the points from the same record are connected by straight-line segments.

Clusters then appear as sheaves of line segments that follow roughly the same path across the figure, at least in some regions. One of the obvious weaknesses of the technique is that there is no natural ordering of the attributes—the order chosen for the visualization may reveal or conceal the presence of clusters.

Most parallel coordinate visualizations also allow a range for one of the attributes to be selected, and all of the lines that intersect that range to be color-coded. This makes the process of cluster discovery interactive since a user can experiment with whether apparent clusters are genuine, whether what appears to be a single cluster at one attribute is actually more than one when other attributes are taken into account and so on. Since the process of selecting clusters is analyst-driven, the number of clusters does not have to be known in advance, but it is possible for small, non-obvious clusters to be missed.

3.2.3 Independent Component Analysis

Independent Component Analysis (ICA) [3, 23–25] is another matrix decomposition, like Singular Value Decomposition, but its properties are different. The structures for which it looks are local, unlike the global variation of SVD, and these local structures can be interpreted as clusters.

An ICA expresses a data matrix, A, as the product:

$$A = WH$$

where, if A is $n \times m$, W is $n \times k$ and H is $k \times m$ for some parameter k less than the minimum of n and m. As with SVD, the rows of matrix H can be interpreted as new "axes" and the entries of the rows of W as coordinates with respect to these axes. However, the rows of H are not orthogonal so this gives a useful, but not entirely accurate, interpretation.

The algorithm to compute an ICA chooses new axes in directions along which the distribution of the data is far from Gaussian. In practice, this tends to pick out directions in which there are (often small) strongly differentiated sets of points, that is clusters whose "cross section" is quite different from that of a normal or Gaussian distribution. The clusters that ICA finds, therefore, are different from those found by SVD and also from density-based clusters.

The clearest way to interpret an ICA is to regard the columns of the W matrix as defining the strength of membership of each record in k possible clusters. A particular record may be a member of more than one cluster, although this soft membership can be made into a hard one by imposing a cutoff on the strength of association between each record and cluster pair.

Like many clustering algorithms, a weakness of ICA is the need to specify the parameter k, the expected number of clusters, beforehand.

3.2.4 Latent Dirichlet Allocation

Latent Dirichlet Allocation (LDA) [5] can be considered an extension to biclustering, where a soft clustering on the attribute space induces a clustering on the records. It has almost exclusively been applied to extracting topics from sets of documents, but there is no reason why it cannot be used for other data, as long as the entries in the dataset are non-negative and it makes sense to normalize by rows so that the row sums are ones.

Standard clustering algorithms consider attributes as an undifferentiated set. Biclustering algorithms consider attributes as divided into subsets (usually disjoint), with one subset associated with each bicluster. LDA considers attributes as drawn from some set of latent clusters, so that each cluster is a distribution over the attributes. In other words, each cluster depends on all of the attributes but each one relies on each attribute with a different weight. This is a kind of soft clustering of the attributes.

Given a dataset, LDA learns both the number and properties of these latent clusters on the attributes, and from them a soft clustering of the records. If k clusters are discovered, then the output of the clustering algorithm is an $n \times k$ matrix giving the probability of each record's membership in each cluster, and a $k \times m$ matrix giving the probability of each attribute's membership in each cluster. Both of these matrices can be used to generate a hard clustering by, for example, allocating a record to the cluster for which its membership probability is greatest.

3.3 Algorithms that Find Clusters and Their Relationships

Algorithms that not only find clusters and allocate records to them, but also provide some information about how these clusters relate to one another, are more useful. They provide a starting point for building the skeleton.

3.3.1 Clusters Based on Distance

The most direct distance-based clustering algorithm is called k-means [37]. The algorithm first selects k random points in the space spanned by the attributes as potential cluster centroids. The distance of each data point to these centroids is computed, and each point is allocated to its nearest centroid. The mean of the points allocated to each centroid is then computed and this becomes the new cluster centroid. Distances to these new centroids have changed, so all distances are recomputed, and data points reallocated to their nearest centroid. This process of alternately allocating data points to their nearest centroid and recalculating the centroid of the points in each allocated group is repeated until there is no change.

The algorithm is sensitive to the initial choice of starting centroids, so it is common to improve on this by, for example, selecting k small sets of points from the data, and using the centroids of these sets as the initial centroids. This tends to place the initial centroids in regions where data points are present, and avoids large empty regions.

At the end, each cluster is defined by a centroid, and the members of the cluster are those points that are closer to this centroid than to any other. The clustering partitions the space into a Voronoi diagram, since each cluster has linear boundaries separating it from its neighboring clusters, midway between each pair of centroids.

The cluster centroids are points in the space, and so the similarities between centroids act as surrogates for the relationship between clusters. In this case, similarity is based on Euclidean distance, the same measure used for point-point similarity—this will not be the case for all algorithms. Two centroids that are close represent clusters that are similar. The skeleton is then built from the set of edges connecting the cluster centroids.

3.3.2 Clusters Based on Distribution

Another more principled approach to finding clusters in many settings is to assume that a cluster represents a fundamental property of the system being examined, with some superimposed variation. In other words, a cluster should, in a perfect world, correspond to a set of identical records with a particular set of attribute values. What is actually observed are records that are almost identical; furthermore, many records are highly similar, with frequency decreasing with decreasing similarity. In other words, most records are near the "middle" of a cluster. Such a cluster is well modelled by a probability density function shaped like a Gaussian, and a set of clusters by a mixture of Gaussians. Given a dataset, such a set of Gaussians can be fitted to the data using an algorithm called Expectation-Maximization [16]. It has the same two-phase structure as the k-means algorithm.

Each Gaussian is described by its mean, which defines a cluster center, and its standard deviations in each dimension, which are a surrogate for its extents (perhaps using a probability contour for some chosen value). Initially a set of k Gaussians are chosen with random parameters, although as for k-means some initial cleverness can improve the performance of the algorithm. The fit of each point to each of the Gaussians is then computed, that is how likely is it that a particular point is chosen from each of the distributions. Intuitively, we can then think of each point as being divided into k fractions based on these putative cluster memberships.

In the second phase, each distribution is fitted to the fractional points that have been allocated to it. This results in a change to its parameters: it moves towards the center of this set of fractional points, and its shape changes to reflect their distribution in space.

The allocation exercise for points is now repeated with respect to these new distributions, causing a different set of fractions and allocations; this in turn causes a refitting of the distributions.

This repeated process can be shown to converge (to a local optimum) so the algorithm stops when allocations don't change (much). The result is a set of Gaussians that match the structure in the dataset.

There are some complexities to the practical use of the EM algorithm in high dimensions, especially when the number of records is smaller than the apparent dimensionality of the data [17].

Since each Gaussian has infinite support, the result is a soft clustering, but it can easily be made hard by allocating each point to its nearest Gaussian.

The deeper reasons for the clustering provide more information than in the distance-based case. For example, the relative probabilities of membership in the different clusters identify points that are ambiguously clustered because they have similar membership probabilities in more than one cluster.

Each of the virtual points at the cluster centers have membership probabilities in all of the other clusters. These can be interpreted as the similarities between clusters, and so used to construct a higher-level picture of cluster relationships from which a skeleton can be built. Once again, the cluster-cluster similarity is qualitatively the same kind of measure as the point-point similarity.

3.3.3 Semidiscrete Decomposition

Semidiscrete Decomposition (SDD) [32, 33, 39] is a matrix decomposition method that looks for a different kind of bicluster. Given an $n \times m$ data matrix, A, an SDD finds clusters of entries that have similar magnitude (ignoring their sign) in as many rectilinearly aligned locations as possible. For example, given a matrix like this:

$$\begin{pmatrix} 0\ 5\ 0\ 5 \\ 0\ 5\ 0\ 5 \\ 0\ 5\ 0\ 0 \end{pmatrix}$$

there is a block of 5s in rows 1 and 2, and columns 2 and 4, with average magnitude 5. Increasing the size of the footprint of this cluster by adding in row 3, columns 2 and 4 increases the footprint by 2 but decreases the average magnitude from 5 to $25/6 = 4.16$. Thus each term of the objective function regularizes the other. Once a bicluster of this form is accounted for, the average magnitude is subtracted from the entries in the positions covered by the footprint, and the new bicluster searched for. Since the number of possible footprints is very large, the algorithm actually uses a heuristic.

The decomposition expresses A as

$$A = XDY$$

where X is $n \times k$, D is a diagonal matrix whose entries are non-increasing, and Y is $k \times m$. Unlike previous decompositions we have seen, k need not be smaller than m; and the entries of X and Y are either $-1, 0$, or $+1$. Thus the product of the ith column of X and the ith row of Y defines the footprint of the ith cluster, while the ith entry of the diagonal of D is the average magnitude of the entries in that cluster.

SDD defines a biclustering because each footprint finds regions of similar magnitude across the rows but only for some subset of the columns. For high-dimensional data, especially sparse data, this is powerful.

The basic SDD algorithm does not relate the biclusters to one another. However, there is an interpretation of the columns of X that allows clusters to be connected by a ternary tree that provides a helpful relationship among clusters.

Consider the following matrix:

$$\begin{pmatrix} 5 & 5 & 5 & 5 & 0 & 0 & 0 & 0 \\ 5 & 5 & 5 & 5 & 0 & 0 & 0 & 0 \\ 5 & 5 & 6 & 6 & 1 & 1 & 0 & 0 \\ 0 & 0 & 1 & 1 & 9 & 9 & 8 & 8 \\ 0 & 0 & 1 & 1 & 9 & 9 & 8 & 8 \\ 0 & 0 & 0 & 0 & 8 & 8 & 8 & 8 \\ 0 & 0 & 0 & 0 & 8 & 8 & 8 & 8 \end{pmatrix}$$

The first stage of the decomposition finds the large block in the lower right-hand corner with average magnitude about 8, then the block in the upper left-hand corner with average magnitude close to 5, and then the block in the middle with average magnitude close to 1. So the first three columns of X are:

$$\begin{pmatrix} 0 & 1 & 0 \\ 0 & 1 & 0 \\ 0 & 1 & 1 \\ 1 & 0 & 1 \\ 1 & 0 & 1 \\ 1 & 0 & 0 \\ 1 & 0 & 0 \end{pmatrix}$$

The hierarchical classification arises from considering the contents of each row as the branching for that record. (This is a ternary branching because there could also be -1s in the matrix.) So, at the top level, there are four rows in the right-hand branch, and three rows in the middle branch. Neither branch subdivides at the second level. At the third level the right-hand branch has two records in the middle subbranch, and two records in the right-hand subbranch. The middle branch has one record in the right-hand subbranch, and two in the middle subbranch.

This hierarchical clustering has obscured the structure of the third cluster which has become subdivided over the two higher-level clusters. On the other hand, it has correctly indicated that the records within the two higher-level clusters are different. Although there is little theoretical justification for this hierarchical understanding of SDD, in practice it tends to provide interpretable results [14].

3.3.4 Hierarchical Clustering

Hierarchical clustering [28] emphasizes hierarchy rather than the kind of "flat" clustering we have seen so far.

Initially, each point is regarded as a cluster of size 1. Then, using some appropriate measure, the two most similar clusters are joined together. At each subsequent step, the two most similar clusters are joined together, the process ending when all of the points form a single cluster.

At the joining step, the similarity between all pairs of clusters must be computed, so the measure used must generalize to compute this, not just the similarity between points. A large number of such measures have been suggested: for example, the distance between the two closest points in the two clusters, the distance between the two furthest-apart points in the two clusters, or the average distance between pairs of points, one from each cluster.

One of the advantages of hierarchical clustering is that the number of clusters does not have to be specified in advance. Rather, the structure revealed by the clustering can help to suggest how many clusters are present. A simple way to turn a hierarchical clustering into a "flat" clustering is to draw the hierarchical clustering as a tree, where the earlier cluster joins appear near the leaves and the later ones near the root; and then draw a horizontal line at any height. Drawing the line near the leaves produces many clusters; drawing it near the root produces only a few.

Each join of two subclusters to produce a new cluster can also be labelled by the distance between the two subclusters, so an alternative way to produce a flat clustering is to choose a distance threshold and consider a subtree as a cluster as long as its internal joins were of distances below the threshold.

Because distances increase with height in the tree (towards the root) clusterings necessarily consistent of "leaf" clusters connected by networks of edges.

Different choices of similarity measure produce different clusterings, so this should really be considered a family of clustering algorithms.

3.3.5 Minimum Spanning Tree with Collapsing

Minimum spanning tree clustering algorithms superficially resembles hierarchical clustering, except that, within a spanning tree, connections are always between pairs of points while, in hierarchical clustering, connections are always between clusters.

Initially, the two closest points are joined; then, at each subsequent step, the two remaining closest points are joined until all of the points have been connected into a tree. Since similarity is only applied between pairs of points, only a base point-point similarity, usually distance, is required.

Naive minimal spanning tree algorithms are expensive because they require calculating the distance (similarity) between all pairs. Clever algorithms have been developed to reduce this complexity, the current front-runner being the March-Ram-Gray algorithm [38] that has running time very close to $\mathcal{O}(n \log n)$ for n records.

The resulting spanning tree can be converted to a clustering by allocating points to the same cluster whenever their pairwise similarity is sufficiently large (they are connected by sufficiently short edges). Unlike the hierarchical clustering case, the resulting clustering can be a tree of clusters. The skeleton structure connecting the clusters is the collection of edges representing similarities too low (too long) for the threshold, and so comes for free from the clustering.

3.4 Overall Process for Constructing a Skeleton

The overall process for constructing a skeleton uses the following stages:

1. Assume the space spanned by the attributes as the natural geometry for the dataset—so the space has dimensionality m;
2. Represent each record in the dataset by a point in this space, at the positions determined by its attribute values—so the space is occupied by n points;
3. Compute similarities between each pair of points in the natural geometry—to respect the geometry, similarity should almost always be a metric;
4. Use the algorithms we have discussed and the pairwise similarities to discover the clusters in the geometry.

These clusters also need to be connected to one another to form a skeleton, but we postpone the discussion of how this is done to Chap. 5.

Actually this process is quite weak because it does not make full use of the available data, and because similarity in high-dimensional spaces is hard to work with. It is much more powerful to insert a step 2a:

2a. Project the natural geometry into a lower-dimensional space—which has the effect of mapping the points to new positions.

A random projection with good properties addresses the second issue: dealing with similarities in high-dimensional space. Using a semantic projection such as SVD also addresses the first issue, since the data itself is used inductively to determine *which* lower-dimensional space to choose so that the structure in the data is most faithfully retained.

This approach of choosing a space, projecting it to lower dimensions in a data-dependent way, computing pairwise similarities, and then clustering is not the only possible path to construct a representation of the data and a skeleton. We will see in Chap. 6 another construction that begins with pairwise similarity and only then constructs a geometry.

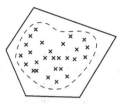

Fig. 3.1 Wrapping a single cluster with two different boundaries, each of which then considers different new points as aberrant

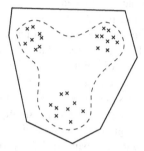

Fig. 3.2 When there are multiple clusters, different kinds of boundaries magnify the differences in how regions are regarded

3.5 Algorithms that Wrap Clusters

We now turn to considering how to capture and describe empty space. Finding empty space means finding and understanding the edges of clusters, that is where each cluster ends and so empty space begins. This requires algorithms that somehow wrap a cluster with a boundary that delimits the two regions—the inside and the outside.

An important issue is how tight such a wrapping should be. Any cluster is derived from a finite part of a finite dataset and almost always there is more data that could have been collected. With extra data, the apparent edges of most clusters would change slightly. Therefore, wrapping a cluster tightly is a kind of overfitting. It's better to generalize each cluster's boundary to reflect the finite basis of its construction. In other words we want new but aberrant data points to fall inside such boundaries so that we do not constantly find them interesting. Figure 3.1 illustrates how different choices of boundary properties (for example, smoothness) make wrappings of different tightness possible.

Another important distinction is whether we are wrapping a set of points that is plausibly represented as a single cluster, or a set that is represented by multiple clusters. This latter case, shown in Fig. 3.2, arises because we want to construct a boundary around an entire dataset to separate ordinary from novel records.

The algorithms we will discuss vary by how smooth the boundaries they construct are, and whether these boundaries depend on all of the points in a cluster, or only on those points that are on the "outside" shell of the cluster.

3.5.1 Distance-Based

The obvious way to construct a distance-based wrapping of a cluster is to construct its convex hull. This implicitly claims that clusters should be convex, that is roughly elliptical; or, equivalently, that records whose attributes are linear combinations of the attributes of the current set of points should also fall in the same cluster.

A convex hull is a reasonable wrapper for a set of points from a single cluster in many settings. It is less clear that it is plausible when wrapping multiple clusters, since it is almost certainly not the case that an entire dataset is approximately convex in the statistical geometry (as illustrated in Fig. 3.2).

A similar, but smoother, boundary can be constructed using the minimum enclosing ellipse of a set of points. The smoothness of an ellipse boundary makes it a kind of generalization of the actual set of points in a cluster. One advantage of using an enclosing ellipse is that it generates a centroid for the cluster, which a convex hull does not. As for a convex hull, it is less plausible to enclose a set of clusters by an ellipse.

Both convex hulls and enclosing ellipses depend only on the extremal points for their shape and position, and so ignore the number, density, and positions of internal points. Both have a natural way to be expanded slightly to produce a looser wrapping if desired.

3.5.2 Distribution-Based

Modelling a cluster by a distribution implicitly assumes that pairwise similarity of points is less important than the relative positions of *all* of the points in the cluster—usually denser towards the "middle", becoming less dense with increasing distance from this "middle". The wrapping is defined as a probability density contour of the distribution fitted to the points of the cluster. This has some advantages: the cluster model is derived from all of the points in the cluster rather than just the extremal points; density is taken into account in a natural way; and the tightness of the wrapping is easy to adjust by choosing a different contour value. Although Gaussians are by far the most common distributions used in practice, other distributions are possible without any substantial change in algorithms.

Using a distribution to model a collection of clusters is more problematic, since these are best represented by a mixture of distributions, for which a single-distribution fit is almost guaranteed to be poor.

3.5.3 1-Class Support Vector Machines

A more flexible way to wrap a cluster is to use a 1-class version of Support Vector Machines [47]. The choice of kernel allows the boundary to be constructed with varying degrees of tightness and curvature ("crinkliness"). 1-class SVMs depend only on the extremal points of the cluster (those that form the support vectors).

Although they are not usually used this way, 1-class SVMs also wrap multiple clusters in a way that reflects what we might want intuitively. If the wrapping is not too tight, the boundary goes around the "outside" of the clusters but dips in between them so that the total enclosed space is much smaller than the convex hull derived from the clusters. The dashed line in Fig. 3.2 is typical of what is produced by a 1-class SVM.

In fact, if the 1-class SVM is tight enough it will wrap each of the component clusters independently. In other words, although the clusters are wrapped with a single enclosing boundary in the higher-dimensional space derived from the kernel, this boundary breaks up into a set of enclosing boundaries when projected into the original data space. This is problematic, since it might be difficult to detect that this has happened.

Although 1-class SVMs are theoretically well founded, the actual boundaries built for real datasets seem to very sensitive to the parameter values chosen (and such choices are hard to make in a principled way).

3.5.4 Autoassociative Neural Networks

All of the previous techniques construct an explicit boundary between the "inside" and the "outside" of a cluster. Autoassociative Neural Networks (AANNs) [4] instead provide a computational test for whether a given data point is in or out. A boundary can be inferred from this test, but the process is essentially reversed compared to the other techniques we have discussed.

An autoassociative neural network is a three-layer network. Its input and output layers are both of size m while the middle layer is usually much smaller. The network is trained in the conventional way (that is, using backpropagation) to replicate its inputs on its outputs. The presence of the small middle layer forces generalization rather than simple copying.

When the network is trained, records that resemble those on which it was trained (that is, records that are "inside" the cluster) are recreated on the outputs with small error. Records that are unlike the training records are reproduced with larger errors and are therefore considered to lie "outside" the cluster. Furthermore, the size of the reproduction error can be interpreted as a surrogate for how "far" the record is outside the cluster.

Such a network is non-linear so that the implicit boundary that it learns can wrap clusters whose natural boundary is complex, and so is poorly modelled by the other techniques we have discussed. The drawback is that training an AANN is comparatively expensive.

When the goal is to wrap a collection of clusters, AANNs can still be used, but in a different form. Using a middle layer that is larger than the input and output layers allows the AANN to reproduce the process used to learn a single cluster for

Fig. 3.3 A covering approach to wrapping a cluster

a set of clusters [6]. Each internal node learns some property of one of the clusters. Although such an AANN could simply replicate its input on its output, and ignore the extra middle-layer neurons, there is nothing in the learning algorithm that makes this arrangement any more likely than any other, and it tends not to happen in practice.

3.5.5 *Covers*

Another way to build a wrapper is to cover each individual data point with a small geometric region, perhaps a sphere or hypercube. The boundary of the union of these individual regions is taken to be the boundary of the cluster. Every point used in the construction is inside this boundary; but the boundary is slightly expanded because of the size of the individual regions. The difficulty is to know what shape and how large to make the regions around each point. Figure 3.3 shows a simple cover approach for a cluster of points that is far from being convex, with each point covered by a small square, and the boundary of the entire cluster constructed from the union of the outer edges of the individual squares. A new point, to be considered as part of the cluster, cannot be too different from at least one of the existing points.

The covering approach is a local generalization of the points from which it is built. Its limitations can be seen by considering how it would work for a set of clusters. It can only cover each of the clusters as if they were independent; it has no way to generalize a covering over all of the clusters (unless the local regions are made very large).

These are by no means all of the possible algorithms that could be used to wrap clusters. Wrapping individual clusters, as we shall see, is the way to begin to understand the structure of empty space between them. Wrapping a set of clusters is the way to distinguish between the kind of data described by a dataset, and all of the other possible data that could exist for the same set of attributes.

3.6 Algorithms to Place Boundaries Between Clusters

Empty space is not just a uniform region, but has a structure all of its own. Moreover, this structure can tell us a lot about the dataset. One important part of this is that points, and regions, close to the boundaries between clusters are especially interesting. Therefore we will need algorithms that can construct such boundaries.

These boundaries are different from those that wrap individual clusters. Wrapping boundaries depend only on points of one particular kind, those that lie within the cluster; and so they tend to wrap each cluster relatively tightly. Boundaries that distinguish between two different kinds of records aim to construct generalized representations of the difference, and so such boundaries tend to lie "midway" between the clusters, and so not necessarily close to either. In other words, such boundaries correspond to predictors trained on the difference between two clusters, considered as two classes.

There are many, many predictors known but we concentrate on two of the strongest, support vector machines (SVMs) and Random Forests.

3.6.1 Support Vector Machines

Support vector machines [13, 15] build boundaries between two classes (in our case, usually one cluster and the rest of the dataset) by constructing the maximal margin separator. In other words, the constructed boundary is the midline of the thickest possible block that can be inserted between the points of the two classes. Obviously, therefore, the position of the boundary depends only on the points from the two classes that face each other in the space, the points that are, in a sense, the closest of each class to the other.

This is important when building a boundary between one class and all of the others because it means that distant clusters do not affect the placement of the boundary—and this seems intuitively appealing.

SVMs have two other significant benefits. First, it is possible to weaken the objective function (finding the thickest block that separates the two classes) by allowing points from either class to be inside it, but with a penalty added to the function that is being minimized. Hence, a boundary can still be built for classes that are not cleanly separable.

Second, the use of the "kernel trick" allows a (smoother, perhaps linear) boundary to be constructed in a higher-dimensional space spanned by combinations of the original attributes. This boundary is then effectively projected into the space spanned by the original attributes where its shape is complex, but tests for which side a given point falls can be made in the higher-dimensional space where they are simple and fast.

3.6.2 Random Forests

Random forests [8, 9] are a generalized ensemble predictor using decision trees [10, 44] as the base predictor.

Given a dataset, an out-of-bag sample (uniformly random with replacement) of the records is selected. A decision tree is built using these records but with one important variation: at each internal node, a fresh set of *mtry* attributes are selected for evaluation and the most predictive used to generate the test at that node. A large set of these modified decision trees are built from fresh samples of the records and used as an ensemble predictor; that is, when a new record is to be classified, the predictions of all of the trees are computed and the overall winner determined by the plurality of the individual predictions.

Random forests are strong predictors. The choice of the attribute tested at each internal node is doubly contextualized, depending on both the comparator set of records *and* of attributes, so individual trees are highly independent in their predictions. All ensemble techniques tend to perform well because the biases of individual predictors cancel each other out, but the independence of random forest trees makes this especially effective.

As with any ensemble, the strength of the vote for the winning class can be interpreted as a surrogate for how strongly the record belongs to that class, that is how far it is from the virtual boundary between the classes. (Since each individual tree defines its own boundary there is no actual boundary for the random forest.)

3.7 Overall Process for Constructing Empty Space

The empty space is derived from the same process that is used to build the skeleton, but comes, of course, from the absence of data, and so of skeleton structure. The empty space exists in the same geometry, usually a lower-dimensional space built from that spanned by the attributes. However, the empty space is not unstructured, but has its own structure, a kind of negative of the skeleton.

First the empty structure is divided into two regions: the region occupied by the data, containing the entire skeleton, and the region "outside" of this, where no meaningful points from the dataset occur. The boundary separating these two regions (which we call the outer boundary) delineates the region where data does or might plausibly exist, and the region where data, if it exists, is considered to be independent of the system under investigation (considered novel or random). Such a boundary is necessary because a high-dimensional space has a large volume, and it is highly unlikely that any real dataset, even a very large one, occupies all of this volume. Delineating the outside region also provides interpretation for new data records in a dynamic setting, suggesting their relevance (inside) or irrelevance (outside).

Several of the wrapping algorithms discussed in the previous sections can be used to create this outer boundary. The construction is non-trivial because most wrapping algorithms are designed to wrap a single, coherent cluster and their behavior on a collection of clusters is not necessarily to compute the intuitively desired outer boundary. There is also an issue about how tightly such an outer boundary should wrap an entire dataset given that almost any dataset is a finite sample of a potentially larger and at least slightly more variable set of data.

Second, within the outer boundary there is also structure to the empty space. Locations, and regions, that are midway between clusters are particularly interesting, for two reasons. Existing records that lie near such locations are most ambiguous in their relationships to the larger structure. Also, new data that falls into such regions has the greatest implications for the existing structure. Such regions are found by building predictors trained on one cluster versus the others.

3.8 Summary

In this chapter, we have introduced four different classes of algorithms that have a role to play in understanding high-dimensional spaces. Projections are a way to reduce the apparent dimensionality of the natural geometry of a dataset. Although projection seems, on the face of it, to discard information and therefore to be a poor first step, two properties make it attractive. First, many datasets, perhaps most, have less underlying dimensionality than they appear to have because the choice of attributes is rarely made in a principled, let alone minimalist, way. The number of ways in which the data can actually vary, the number of latent factors that underlie it, is often much smaller than the number of ways in which it can apparently vary. Second, some of the small-scale variation in a dataset can plausibly be considered as some kind of "noise"—really unmodelled processes—and so projecting away that variation creates a dataset in which the variations of interest are more clearly visible.

Clustering algorithms are the heart of understanding high-dimensional spaces, integrating local, pairwise similarity information into a more-abstract structure of clusters. Each clustering algorithm makes assumptions about what local similarity is like, and how records must fit together to form a cluster. This includes properties such as how large a cluster must be, and what "shape" (in its most general sense) a cluster must be. Most clustering algorithms must also be told how many clusters to look for, which creates another bootstrap problem, since this is not usually obvious when a dataset is first encountered. As usual, this problem is addressed by iteration, trying different numbers of clusters and making a judgement about which seems to produce the best results.

Although clustering algorithms aggregate the records they are given into clusters, the boundaries associated with these clusters are often left ambiguous. In other words, a clustering algorithm identifies which points are "in" the cluster but does not necessarily provide a basis for deciding how similar a novel record/point has to be to be considered as also being inside the cluster. We therefore described several ways in which a cluster can be wrapped to give it an explicit boundary. This boundary then takes on a life of its own, and becomes an abstraction of the cluster independent of the particular points from which it was built.

Finally, predictors provide a boundary or decision surface between points belonging to one class and points belonging to another. When clusters are interpreted as classes, and so cluster membership provides class labels, these boundaries lie in the empty space between clusters, and so provide a semantics for regions of empty space.

Chapter 4
Spaces with a Single Center

The intuitive view of the natural space created from large data is that it somehow looks as shown in Fig. 4.1.

In the center are the most common, normal, or typical records and they all resemble each other to some extent; outside this are records that are more scattered and less normal or typical, resembling each other less; and outside this are records that are much more scattered, much less frequent, and very untypical. The reason that this structure seems intuitively appealing is that, as records become inherently more unusual (further from the center), they also become less alike (because of the different directions). Much research has assumed a space something like this, although often implicitly, for example much of the work on *outlier detection*.

However, the assumption has only to be made explicit to reveal how assailable it is—there is usually no particular reason why data should be clustered around a single center, and every reason to expect a more complex structure (see Chap. 5). Nevertheless, the single-center assumption makes a useful framework within which to consider approaches to understanding skeletons and empty space in high-dimensional datasets.

4.1 Using Distance

Note that the intuitive model of space is implicitly a *distance-based* one: points that are near the center are normal, and abnormality increases with distance from the center. Also the model assumes that the center of the cloud of data points is at the origin; but this will usually only be true if some normalization has been applied to the data. For example, many kinds of datasets describing human activity involve only non-negative numbers (financial amounts, purchases made, phone minutes used, ages) so the center of the data cloud for such datasets will be somewhere in the positive hyperquadrant unless normalization is applied.

If distance from the center is used as the only criterion then all of the records can be ranked on this basis, and the most distant one labelled as the most anomalous,

D. B. Skillicorn, *Understanding High-Dimensional Spaces*, SpringerBriefs in Computer Science, DOI: 10.1007/978-3-642-33398-9_4, © The Author 2012

Fig. 4.1 An intuitive view of
a space with a single center

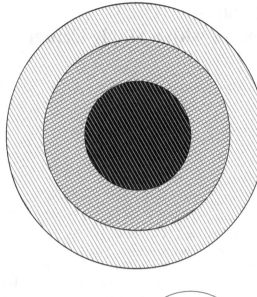

Fig. 4.2 Ranking extremal
points by distance from the
center conceals big differences

while those closest to the center are the most normal. However, a purely distance-based view does not compare records to one another in a meaningful way. Consider Fig. 4.2, in which a ranking of the three outlying points by distance from the origin conceals the fact that, as records, the two disks are quite similar, while the cross is about as different from them as it could be.

Clearly direction, as well as distance, should be taken into account. But it is far from clear how information about this second dimension of direction should be integrated into a simple ranking from most to least anomalous.

4.2 Using Density

A more sophisticated approach is to take into account the *structure* of the center to determine how to consider the structure of outlying points. In other words, it makes more sense to consider how far a point is *from other points* than from some notional center of the entire data cloud.

Fig. 4.3 Two "outlying" points that are close to the center

In Chap. 3, we saw a number of ways in which a cluster can be wrapped. One simple way is to fit an m-dimensional Gaussian to the entire set of data points. The probability associated with each point can then be interpreted as an inverse distance—points with low probability are considered outliers. This is not equivalent to simply computing distance from the center because the shape of the Gaussian itself depends on how the points are distributed. The Gaussian will have greater extent in dimensions that are occupied richly by data points so that it is "harder" to be anomalous in such dimensions.

Another approach is to compute the distances from each point to its kth nearest neighbors, usually for some k of about 10. We can't tell, in advance, which other points are likely to be fairly near neighbors of the point we're considering, so this almost always requires the full n^2 distance computations. A number of indexing schemes have been suggested to allow rough estimates of which other points are near and which are far, but these often conceal an expensive dependency on the dimensionality of the space and so do not help in practice.

With this information, a number of ways of ranking are possible. For example, records can be ranked in order of the distance to the kth of their k nearest neighbors. For points that are in dense regions and so close to many other points, this distance will always be small. However, for points that are in emptier regions of the space, whether they are far from the origin or not, these distances will be large, and especially large for isolated points. This is related to the idea of local outliers [11].

Figure 4.3 shows a situation where points might reasonably be considered as outlying, even though they are closer to the center than many of the other points.

Even more information can be extracted from the data about near neighbors. For example, a point all of whose k neighbors are far away is clearly isolated. Other points may have a few close neighbors, with the remainder far away; such a point is a member of a small outlying cluster. Other (most) points will have all of their k neighbors close. In general, a plot of distance as a function of position in the list of nearest neighbors reveals much about the local neighborhood of each point. While this might be too expensive to compute for all of the points, it is worth doing to understand the different properties of outliers.

It is also possible to create the convex hull of the points and then shrink it slightly. Points that are now outside the convex hull are outliers. This, however, makes a stronger assumption—convexity—about the shape of the data cloud.

4.3 Understanding the Skeleton

At first glance, the skeleton of a single-center space is trivial to understand—it consists of a single cluster. However, the typical structure of such a single cluster is usually more than just a single ellipse, and so direction becomes important for understanding its structure.

First, projective techniques tend to squash clusters, especially clusters that are not very well separated, into a single cluster.

Second, in many settings clusters are not well-separated, but rather represent degrees of variation, especially when they capture human variability. For example, datasets describing word use or opinions or tastes often have a cluster structure that looks like a set of radial arms from a center. These clusters meet and overlap in the center, where the data records are so bland that they cannot be separated clearly into clusters; while more distinctive records can be. In such cases, the skeleton is a single cluster, but it is helpful to understand its "starfish" structure to understand the data.

Example. *As an example, let us consider a dataset extracted from the U.S. State of the Union addresses, from George Washington to George W. Bush. In particular, this dataset is based on the 3000 most-frequent words in that set of documents.*

Documents are similar when they use the same words with roughly the same frequency. Figure 4.4 shows the result of using singular value decomposition, truncated to two dimensions, and then plotted. The label on each address is the year in which it was given.

In this rendering, there appears to be only a single cluster, but one with three arms that almost, but not quite separate in the center. Somewhat surprisingly, these almost-clusters consist of speeches from different time periods: the upper one the early speeches until about 1870, the right-hand one the speeches until about 1910, and the left-hand one the more recent speeches. Clearly language patterns have changed over time; but what is striking is how suddenly these changes appear to have taken place. It is also surprising that the language patterns of individual presidents (and their staffs) are not more visible.

A different view is shown in Fig. 4.5. This figure shows that the structure is not quite as simple as the previous rendering suggested: there is a clearer separation of the cluster of early speeches, with a distinct subgroup in 1809 and 1810 (Madison); the right-hand cluster has a subgroup covering the years 1899–1912 (McKinley–T. Roosevelt–Taft); and there are hints of further distinctions.

For this data, a random projection into three dimensions, shown in Fig. 4.6, does not show any of the clustered structure shown by the singular value decomposition.

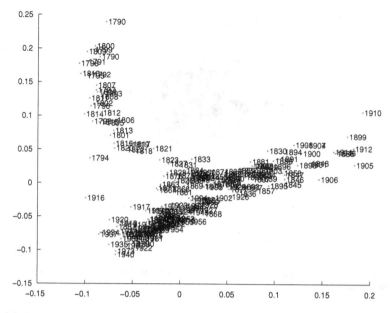

Fig. 4.4 Two-dimensional plot of presidential State of the Union addresses after singular value decomposition

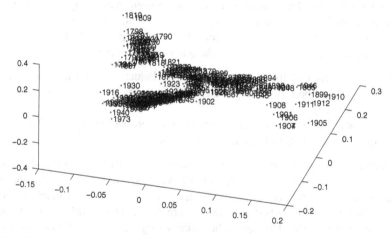

Fig. 4.5 Another view of the plot of State of the Union addresses, using three dimensions

4.4 Understanding Empty Space

In a single-centered space, the empty space is necessarily around the 'outside' of the skeleton. Its role is primarily to define the region in which data points, especially newly arriving data points, are not considered part of the real-world system as it is currently being modelled. Thus it has three roles:

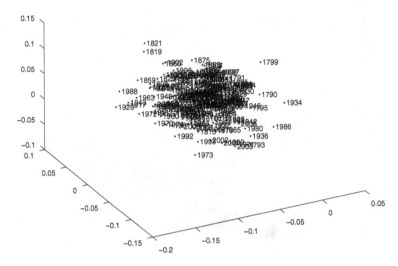

Fig. 4.6 A random projection of the State of the Union addresses into three dimensions, with little apparent structure

- It indicates points in the given data that are so different from the remainder that they should be discounted as noise. The boundary between an anomaly and a point that should be considered noise is always problematic—indeed much of the statistical work in outlier detection aims to detect outliers for the purpose of removing them.
- For newly arriving points that fall in the outer empty region:
  - it may suggest that the current model is inadequate, so that the construction process should be redone (especially as the number of points in this category becomes large);
  - it may suggest problems with the way in which data is being collected and processed that needs to be dealt with upstream.

To define this outer region some kind of boundary needs to be constructed between the records that are understood by the model skeleton, and those (if there are any) that are not. In other words, the boundary may enclose all of the available records, but still define a region outside of these where new points could fall; or it could enclose most of the available records but acknowledge that some of those points do not naturally fit into the skeleton implied by the others.

We have seen (Chap. 3) there are three different kinds of enclosing boundaries:

- Enclosing boundaries derived from the center or centroid of the data. Such boundaries depend on all of the points, but indirectly because the entire set of points determines the center.
- Enclosing boundaries based on the outermost points. Such boundaries ignore the internal structure of the skeleton and use only the extremal (or nearly extremal) points.

- Enclosing boundaries based on local geometry. Such boundaries take the union of structures defined by each of the points, that is they generate some kind of covering.

The role of empty space is to aid understanding by making it clear where data is not, which might itself be revealing; and to provide a way to understand newly arriving data in dynamic systems. Depending on the precise way the boundary is generated and its looseness, data that arrives and is placed outside the boundary is interpreted as qualitatively different to data that falls inside. Such outside records may be ignored with some confidence; but the arrival of many of them may indicate a need to rebuild the current model.

The boundary constructed between the central cluster and the empty space around it will be called the *outer boundary*. Points that lie outside it are considered to be novel points in the hierarchy of significance from Chap. 1. Points that lie well outside it can be considered to be random points.

4.5 Summary

A single-centered space is the simplest example of a high-dimensional space. In such a space, both the skeleton and the empty space are straightforward to understand. The skeleton consists of a single node but, because of the use of projection, the structure of this single node can be complex. Empty space consists of the entire space around the central node, and the entire space is divided into only two regions: the "inside" which contains the skeleton, and the "outside" which contains everything else. The outer boundary which divides these two regions separates novel and random points from normal, and aberrant points. The existence of interesting points remains ambiguous. It is possible to define them by using two outer boundaries, of differing sophistication and tightness—but the existence of a substantial region between two such boundaries hints that the space is actually multicentric, a theme we take up in Chap. 5.

Chapter 5
Spaces with Multiple Centers

The assumption that, in a natural geometry, spaces derived from data have a single center with a single cluster is implicitly an assumption that there is one underlying process responsible for generating the data, and that the spatial variation around some notional center is caused by some variation overlaying this process. Often, perhaps most of the time, it is much more plausible that there are multiple, interacting processes generating the data, and so at least multiple clusters. Each of these clusters might have a notional center with some variation around it, but there is typically also some relationship among the clusters themselves. In other words, the skeleton for such data must describe both the clusters and the connections. The analysis is significantly more complex, but more revealing.

To continue the tax example, the characteristic tax return structures across an entire community are not just affected by each individual's total amount of income, but also how that income is earned. It might well be the case that there is a single large cluster describing taxpayers who work a single job and have tax deducted in a standard way—this cluster might be quite elongated to reflect the fact that incomes vary substantially even within this category. However, there are likely to be other clusters of taxpayers who are self-employed, and therefore have different patterns of income and deductions, retired people, those who live on investment income, and many other qualitatively different categories as well. Trying to model data like this as if it is single centered cannot represent the structure adequately.

The high-level global strategy for understanding these multicentric spaces is as follows:

- Find the clusters present in the data;
- Discover the relationships among the clusters to produce a skeleton for the given data;
- Analyze the empty space to define an outer region that is not part of the data being modelled (as we did in the single-centered case);
- Model the empty space *between* the clusters to understand its structure.

D. B. Skillicorn, *Understanding High-Dimensional Spaces*, SpringerBriefs in Computer Science, DOI: 10.1007/978-3-642-33398-9_5, © The Author 2012

5.1 What is a Cluster?

The first step of this process is to discover the clusters present in the data. In the single-centered case, identifying a cluster was straightforward—a cluster is the entire set of data, perhaps except for a few extremal points. In a multicentric setting, the problem of identifying a cluster becomes more difficult. Somehow a cluster must be a set of points that are more similar than average, perhaps surrounded by a region in which there are few points.

Some of the possible criteria for what makes a cluster are:

- Size—a cluster contains at least a certain number of points.
- Density—a cluster contains points that are sufficiently close to one another (which immediately introduces subquestions: minimum closeness, average closeness, or variable closeness in different parts of the cluster).
- Shape—a cluster has to be roughly elliptical, or perhaps has to be more spider-like, or can be defined by some other more abstract property.

A more subtle and troublesome issue is whether clusters have to have the same properties anywhere in the space, or whether size and density might be different in different regions. Homogeneity is usually assumed, but there are many settings where that is an implausible assumption. In essence, homogeneity is an implicit claim that similarity means the same thing even among subsets of records that are themselves very different.

Example. *In the example in the previous chapter, we saw that some kinds of data have a global center, although the structure around this center is not usually a sphere or ellipse—rather it can have arms, each of which extends from the center, and could be considered a kind of cluster.*

Many other kinds of data do not have such an obvious center, or even a center at all; and so the structure overall is more complex. Figure 5.1 illustrates a dataset of Internet traffic, with 14 attributes capturing properties of connection sessions. The plot shows the records, one per session, after a projection to two dimensions using singular value decomposition.

The figure shows that there is a large central cluster; but the structure around it is complex, with several smaller clusters, and many outlying isolated points. It shows how difficult the problem of understanding a dataset can be, and is very different from the motivating example datasets that often appear in outlier detection papers.

Figure 5.2 shows the labelling induced by computing the local outlier score for each data point. High scoring points are mostly those that are isolated, but even the presence of a few points in a region is enough to reduce the local outlier scores of nearby points. The local outlier scores are calculated in the original 14-dimensional space, while the rendering uses only the most significant two dimensions of the SVD. Nevertheless, it seems surprising that the points at the extreme left-hand side are considered less outlying than those closer to the middle. Real datasets have complex local-outlier-score structure that makes it difficult to decide which points are interesting outliers.

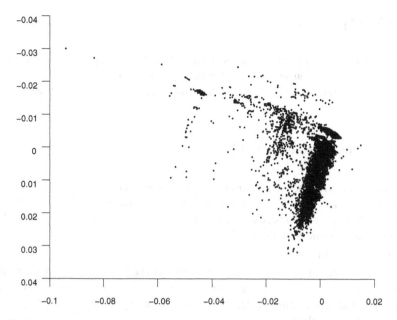

Fig. 5.1 Internet sessions projected into two dimensions using singular value decomposition

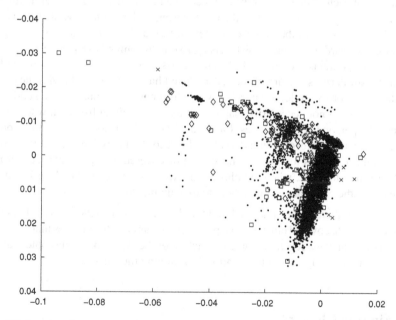

Fig. 5.2 Local outlier scores overlaid on the same SVD projection: *dot* score less than 2; *square* score between 2 and 3; *cross* score between 3 and 4; and *diamond* score greater than 4. Because the calculation is purely local, anomalous points appear in many different parts of the plot, and there is no way to compare them to each other in the global context

5.2 Identifying Clusters

Once we have decided what properties clusters should have, or perhaps have decided to postpone this decision and see what kinds of structures emerge from the data, there are several different ways in which clusters can be discovered and identified.

5.2.1 Clusters Known Already

The easiest way is when the data already has associated class labels. When this happens, then each class label is associated, by definition, with one cluster. Nevertheless, it may be worth executing one of the cluster discovery algorithms on the data to assess the robustness of the labelling.

There are three possibilities:

1. There is a 1-to-1 match between clusters and labels, that is each cluster contains records all of which have the same class label. This is obviously the best scenario and provides convincing evidence that the "meaning" of each cluster has been captured by the classes.
2. More than one cluster contains records with the same class label, but all of the records in each of these clusters have the same label. This suggests that membership of this class arises for more than one reason, each reason associated with one of the clusters. The labelling is consistent with the clustering, but it is no longer straightforward to use the class labels to assign "meaning" to each cluster.
3. A cluster contains records with different class labels. This is entirely possible, for the similarity structure of the records need have nothing to do with the class labelling. For example, a natural way to cluster people would be by gender— but this would not necessarily match with a class labelling based on whether or not each person liked anchovies. Labels could have been associated with records on the basis of information external to the records themselves, or on the basis of similarity that is too weak to have been discovered by a particular clustering algorithm. However, when the cluster structure and the class labels crosscut in this way, the class labels do not help to explain the "meaning" of clusters.

In any case, there is the option to build the skeleton based on the labels or to build it based on the discovered clusters. The presence of class labels indicates that the data is understood at some level, but the construction of the skeleton still has potential to reveal extra knowledge about the relationships among the classes.

5.3 Finding Clusters

In Chap. 3, we saw some algorithms (Sect. 3.2) that can be used to discover clusters when they are not already known.

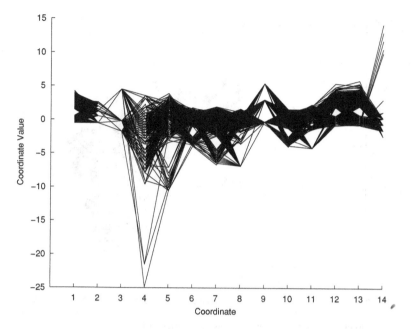

Fig. 5.3 Parallel coordinates view of Internet sessions data

The first decision to make is whether to look for clusters in the natural geometry, or to use projective techniques to first reduce the dimensionality. In general, projective techniques, especially inductive ones, make it easier to see structure in the data, and so should be used first.

Cluster discovery algorithms were divided into two groups. The first group are those that discover individual clusters without finding the relationships among them. These include:

- Density-based techniques;
- Analyst-guided techniques such as parallel coordinates;
- Independent Component Analysis;
- Latent Dirichlet Allocation.

Choosing between these techniques is a decision about what kind of clusters are expected in the data: a certain kind of spidery cluster for density-based techniques, small clusters with sharp edges for ICA, and so on. This is difficult in practice since it is seldom clear, at the beginning, what kind of clusters might be present in a particular dataset. It might be necessary to use a few different algorithms and look at the results before selecting the best (that is, the most revealing). Many clustering algorithms produce similar results for the top-level or largest clusters, but disagree about the smaller, finer-scale structure.

Example. *Figure* 5.3 *shows parallel coordinates applied to the Internet sessions dataset. There is some evidence of three clusters from the values of attribute 9, and*

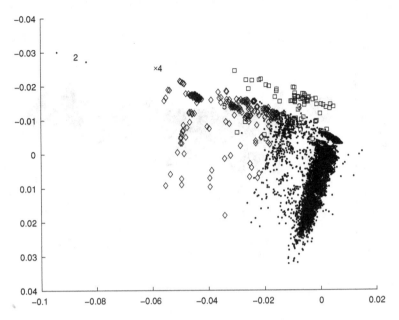

Fig. 5.4 Internet sessions dataset—allocations to 5 clusters using k-means

some obvious outliers from the values of attribute 4, but it is hard to draw deeper conclusions.

The second group are techniques that discover clusters but in such a way that the relationships among the clusters are at least partially revealed. These include:

- Distance-based techniques such as k-means;
- Distribution-based techniques such as Expectation-Maximization;
- Semidiscrete Decomposition;
- Hierarchical clustering, followed by collapsing of levels;
- Minimum Spanning Tree, followed by collapsing of short edges.

The first two techniques compute a complete graph of the clusters, that is the relationship between every pair of clusters is or can be computed. In contrast, the last three techniques construct a tree of relationships among clusters.

Choosing a technique requires some knowledge, or at least expectation, of what clusters will be like. Since these techniques also build some structure among the clusters, considerations of what this structure might be like are also relevant to choosing a technique.

Example. *Figure 5.4 shows the results of clustering the Internet sessions data using the k-means algorithm with 5 clusters (using the projected positions for each session). Each cluster is displayed using a different symbol for its points. The cluster centers are shown by numbers: cluster 1 lies in the middle of the large cluster of dots; cluster 2 lies at the extreme left; cluster 3 lies among the squares; cluster 4 appears to be a single cross; and cluster 5 lies among the diamonds.*

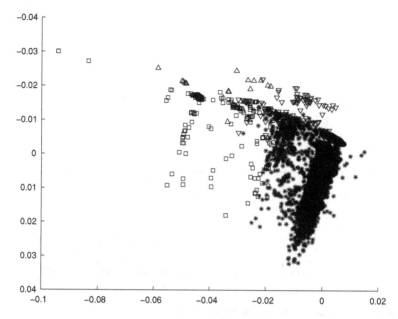

Fig. 5.5 Internet sessions data—semidiscrete decomposition hierarchical clustering for the *top* two levels: −1, +1 (*diamond*), −1, 0 (*down triangle*), −1, −1 (*up triangle*), 0, −1 (*square*), 0, 0 (*star*), 0, +1 (*plus*). The two points at the extreme *left-hand side* separate from the rest of the squares at the next level

The labelling induced by the k-means clustering algorithm seems consistent with the data in the sense that points that are similar (close together) tend to be allocated to the same cluster. The distance calculations for the k-means algorithm are done in the 14-dimensional space spanned by all of the record attributes.

By experiment, using fewer than 5 clusters matches the large-scale structure well but does not separate the outlying points, while using more clusters begins to divide what appear to be coherent clusters in the plot into subclusters.

Figure 5.5 shows the results of clustering the Internet session data using semidiscrete decomposition. The clustering provides more information than the k-means clustering because we know that the clusters involving diamonds and triangles are related; and so are the clusters involving stars and squares. Each record in the dataset can be labelled with the entries in the corresponding row of the decomposition matrix, and these labels become cluster identifiers to any desired level of granularity.

Figure 5.6 shows the results of a hierarchical clustering on this dataset (using Euclidean distance and Ward's measure of cluster similarity). A plausible way to create five distinct clusters is shown by the rectangles. The figure also shows how the amount of information implicit in a hierarchical clustering can become overwhelming.

The minimum spanning tree for this data is shown in Fig. 5.7, overlaid on the projection using SVD. This is only a subset of the records; although this is not a very

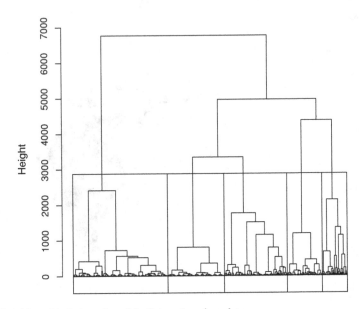

Fig. 5.6 A hierarchical clustering of the Internet sessions data

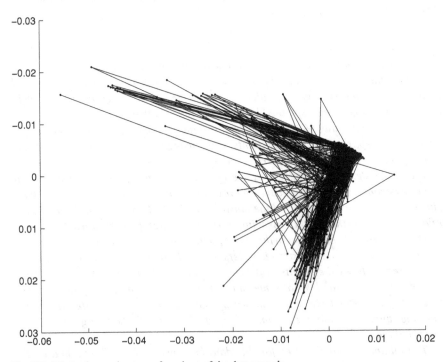

Fig. 5.7 Minimal spanning tree of a subset of the data records

large dataset, the computation and space required to build the pairwise similarities for all of the records exceeds the capability of ordinary computing platforms and tools.

Many of the outlying records are leaves of the spanning tree as expected (even when there are a number of such records that appear quite similar).

5.4 Finding the Skeleton

Once we have found the set of clusters, the next step is to identify the skeleton that relates them. The skeleton is the collection of weighted edges that connect clusters to one another, but the immediate question is: which edges should be included? To put it another way, what kind of graph should the skeleton be?

The obvious answers are:

- The skeleton is the complete (weighted) graph connecting every cluster to every other.
- The skeleton is a tree with weighted edges, the obvious tree to choose being the minimal spanning tree that connects the clusters.

The skeleton must connect the clusters into a single component, since we want to be able to relate any cluster to the global structure that the entire set of clusters captures.

There are obvious advantages to choosing the minimal spanning tree as the skeleton: it represents the core structure of the connections between the clusters, and it provides an easy-to-understand view of this core structure. However, we will see, in Chap. 7, that some kinds of ranking are difficult on such a spanning tree, but possible on the complete graph, so there will be some settings where the complete graph skeleton will be useful.

For those cluster-discovery algorithms that do not relate the clusters to one another (density-based, analyst-driven, ICA, and LDA), building the skeleton remains a non-trivial step. There are several ways in which the relationships among the clusters can be constructed; the issue is whether these mechanisms produce a skeleton that is justifiable and appropriate.

We have examined several algorithms that provide a natural way to connect one cluster to another. Let us now reconsider these for their usefulness for building one or other form of skeleton.

A distance-based clustering algorithm such as k-means provides a distance-based measure of cluster (dis)similarity that applies to all pairs of clusters, based on their centroids. It is therefore straightforward to build the complete graph of clusters. A minimal spanning tree algorithm can then be used to select the spanning tree subset of edges. Since the number of clusters is typically small, the complexity of the MST algorithm is negligible.

A distribution-based clustering algorithm such as Expectation-Maximization also has a natural inter-cluster similarity measure in which the mean of each distribution is regarded as the notional center of each cluster. The similarity between clusters is then the membership probability of each center in all of the other distributions. This creates a complete graph whose edge weights come from these probabilities, and this can be reduced to a minimal spanning tree as usual.

For clusterings based on Semidiscrete Decomposition, distance between clusters depends on distance between the leaves in the ternary tree that defines clusters. This is somewhat complicated by the fact that the records in a $+1$ branch and a -1 branch at the same level are not distinct clusters, but equal and opposite versions of the same cluster. For example, a matrix with rows

$$\begin{pmatrix} 5 & 5\,0\,0 \\ -5 & -5\,0\,0 \\ 0 & 0\,0\,0 \end{pmatrix}$$

generates an X matrix whose first column is $+1, -1, 0$, but the first two rows are not dissimilar, just opposite from the viewpoint of this decomposition. One possible distance measure in the hierarchical tree of clusters is to count distance 0 for a move up or down a 0-labelled edge, since such edges imply no particular relationship between the cluster at one level and the cluster at another; a distance of 1 for a move up or down a $+1$ or -1 labelled edge, except that a move from the $+1$ to the -1 branch *at the same level* should count as 1, not 2. The resulting skeleton is derived from the hierarchical ternary construction but uses extra semantics to alter it. In this case, the "natural" skeleton is a tree. It can be extended to a complete graph using transitivity.

For a hierarchical clustering, chopped off at some height to give a flat clustering, the relationship between the resulting clusters is given by the tree that remains above the point of the cut. The tree itself already contains the order in which the clusters were joined, together with weights derived from the inter-cluster distance that was used to make the join at each level. A spanning tree skeleton is therefore already computed, and can be extended to a complete graph using transitivity.

A minimal spanning tree construction, of course, can be converted into a clustering by collapsing edges shorter than some threshold; the remaining edges provides a spanning tree to serve as the skeleton.

All of these clustering algorithms have some natural extension that acts as a measure of inter-cluster similarity, but they are of two quite different kinds. Distance-based and distribution-based algorithms naturally produce a complete graph, from which a spanning tree can be extracted. SDD, hierarchical clustering, and the minimal spanning tree clustering algorithms all produce a tree, for which the complete graph is the transitive closure. This transitive closure is not necessarily the same as the complete graph that might be constructed in some more direct way, and for certain kinds of rankings this becomes an issue.

We have also seen that there are algorithms that find clusters, but find each one "in isolation", so that is there is no natural way to discover the relationship between clusters in the context of the clustering algorithm. This is an important but little-studied problem. For example, the clusters produced by these algorithms do not have centers or extents in some plausible geometry—cluster membership depends on some more-abstract property.

One family of solutions is known. In hierarchical clustering, the objects that are joined at each stage are clusters, and these clusters can become quite unusual in the last few rounds of the algorithm—because the points they include become increasingly diverse. The similarity measures used in such algorithms therefore work reasonably even for quite odd clusters. There are four common measures that can be generalized to become inter-cluster similarities and only require a cluster to be a defined set of points:

1. Single link—the distance between two clusters is the distance between their closest points;
2. Complete link—the distance between two clusters is the distance between their furthest points;
3. Average—the distance between two clusters is the average of the distances between pairs with one point from each cluster;
4. Ward's measure—the closeness of two clusters is the amount by which the sum of squares of the combined cluster increases relative to the sum of squares of the individual clusters before they are combined.

Each of these choices imposes an implicit structure on the skeleton; for example, using the single-link measure tends to produce long, "skinny" structures, while using the complete-link measure produces more convex structures. The weaknesses, or at least uncertainties, of these ways of connecting standalone clusters is one reason to prefer other clustering algorithms.

The number of clusters is typically much smaller than the number of records (points), so even expensive measures are workable to construct the skeleton from the standalone clusters.

Those techniques that find clusters and also their relationships within a single algorithm are, of course, easier to work with. All of them lift a local, point-point, measure of similarity that is used to find the clusters to a global measure of similarity that defines cluster-cluster similarity. However, subtleties remain.

It is also worth remarking that, in data where the clusters are biclusters, similarity between clusters is not necessarily very well defined. For example, if two biclusters have no overlapping attributes in common (that is, one set of attributes are all zeros for one cluster, and the other set are all zeros for the other), then the dataset can be broken into two independent pieces. Algorithms will compute a similarity between such clusters, but such a similarity must be artificial. Even when two clusters overlap slightly (for example, as in Fig. 2.1 where the clusters overlap only in the vertical direction) the similarity between them depends on attributes that they do not share and so is somewhat misleading. This problem tends to occur in datasets that are sparse and high-dimensional just because of the nature of the data, that is, in such datasets, *all* clusters tend to be biclusters.

5.5 Empty Space

Just as for the single-centered case, the empty space between clusters plays an important role in understanding the data. However, there are now two kinds of empty space, while before there was only one.

The first is the empty space around the entire set of data. As before, the purpose of this space is primarily to make it clear, when new data arrives, whether or not it fits with the existing data and the model built from them. Because the data no longer have a single center, deciding what this region looks like is more difficult than before.

The second is the empty space *between* the clusters, a kind of emptiness that is qualitatively new when there are multiple clusters. Data points in such regions are outliers in a different sense from points that lie outside the entire region of data. Newly arriving data that falls between clusters cannot be ignored as noise—rather they suggest that there are inadequacies with the existing model (clustering).

5.5.1 An Outer Boundary and Novel Data

As before, some data will be so far from the model of the dataset that it is natural to conclude that it arises from some completely different process, and so can be ignored. In the single-centered case, we constructed a boundary around the single cluster that represented the entire data using distances, densities, probability densities, or representational richness. The same repertoire can be applied in the multicentric case, but more care is needed because there is no natural center to a set of clusters.

As before, there are three broad approaches: (a) center-based; (b) boundary-based; and (c) representation-based.

A center-based approach can use distance, density, or probability density, but none of these is entirely appropriate for the multicentric case. For example, suppose we want to use simple distance and enclose the entire dataset (or most of it) in a boundary at a fixed distance. The problem then becomes where to place the center from which this distance is to be calculated. The obvious solution is to use the centroid of the entire set of data. However, this centroid is only the 'center' of the data in a very rough sense, and it is easy to construct datasets where the centroid is quite skewed in the data. It is all too likely that the centroid will be a point in empty space because it represents a global average, and averages over different clusters are like averages over apples and oranges. A typical scenario illustrating the problem is shown in Fig. 5.8.

Using density is also problematic. If we want the set of clusters to become a single cluster that will define the known region of data, then we need to choose a density that is low enough that all of the clusters will merge into a single cluster. However, such a low density will encompass much of the space on the 'outside' of the existing clusters as well, and so new points that are quite far from the known data in some directions may well fall into the known space. The issue cannot be addressed by using different

Fig. 5.8 The centroid (*square*) is not the natural center of the data

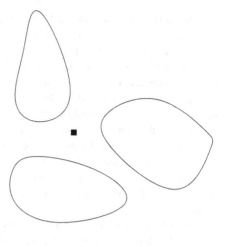

Fig. 5.9 Even though the *circles* and the *squares* have similar density, the *circles* fit within the entire data better than the *squares*

densities in different regions; the desired behavior is that the required density should be lower on the *inside* of clusters (that is, the sides facing other clusters) but higher on the *outside* of clusters. An example is shown in Fig. 5.9.

Finally using a distribution-based approach suffers from both of the problems of distance- and density-based techniques. Such a distribution requires a defined center and it is often not plausible to choose one; and, almost by definition, the distribution is multi-peaked. The temptation is to use a Gaussian around the centroid of the data but this is clearly not going to fit typical data well.

The second approach is to define the outer region based on the boundaries of the existing clusters, that is to ignore the sizes and densities of the points in each cluster. The same three approaches that were used in the single-centered model could be used. For example, a convex hull of the entire set of data points could be constructed. This has the right structure because only the points on the "outside" of each cluster define the surface of the convex hull. The regions linearly between the existing clusters are also within the convex hull; there is a certain plausibility to that.

A more generous outer boundary can be constructed using the minimum volume enclosing ellipse of the entire set of points, more generous because of the smoothness of the boundary. Again, the boundary of the region depends only on the outer points in each of the clusters.

The third approach is to use 1-class Support Vector Machines. These also create a boundary that depends only on the outer points in the dataset, but the boundary can be made to fit the data more or less tightly depending on the kernel used. Some care is needed, since a sufficiently tight boundary will actually wrap each of the clusters independently—the boundary is topologically of genus zero in the higher-dimensional space implied by the kernel, but need not be in the original space of the data. Such a tight boundary does not have the desired property, since points that lie between the clusters are considered outside the outer boundary; but it may imply that the clusters present in the data are very distinct or well-separated which may be relevant to understanding the problem domain.

Techniques based on the outer points of the dataset are attractive because they naturally build on the outer edges of clusters, without having to explicitly compute these outer edges.

Another approach to constructing this outer boundary is to use representational complexity, for example using Auto-associative Neural Networks. The entire dataset is used to train such a network to replicate each given input on its outputs. Because the structure of the known data is a set of separate clusters, it is necessary to use AANNs with a wide hidden layer. An AANN with a small hidden layer must arrange the clusters into a 1-dimensional centralized structure that tends not to fit well with multi-cluster data.

When fully trained, the error in replication is a surrogate for how well any record corresponds to the training data. There is no need even for a virtual center for the collection of clusters—representational complexity addresses the issue in a different way. As for 1-class SVMs, choosing some particular threshold for the acceptable representation error defines a boundary around the data; but choosing this threshold too small creates a boundary that wraps individual clusters rather than the entire set of clusters.

Any one of these techniques defines a boundary around the entirety of the data points that defines the distinction between data that is potentially well modelled by the clustering, and data that should be considered as resulting from some other distinct, unmodelled process. To say it another way, the implication of a new record arriving outside the boundary is that the existing model, that is clustering, may be incomplete, but what there is of it is accurate. A new record arriving inside the boundary has more subtle implications that we now explore.

5.5.2 Interesting Data

Records that lie between the clusters but inside the outer boundary represent data that is not well captured by the clustering, but that is relevant to it. In other words, such data has implications for the correctness of the clustering, suggesting that a pair of clusters may in fact be a single one with the isolated point the only instance of data so far filling in the gap; or suggesting that there is another cluster present in the data for which the isolated point is, so far, the only member.

Fig. 5.10 Points with different significance (*dashed line
is the outer boundary*)

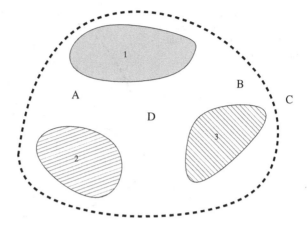

There is also the issue of which cluster or clusters an isolated point should be viewed as associated with, and so modifying. Figure 5.10 shows some possible locations for isolated points.

A point such as A lies midway between clusters 1 and 2 and so suggests, weakly, that clusters 1 and 2 might be the same cluster, or that there is another cluster between them. New data that falls close to A would increase the likelihood of one or other of these hypotheses. In contrast, point B is close to cluster 3. It suggests that cluster 3 might have a greater extent on its upper side than the present clustering indicates, but it is less interesting than point A. Note point C which, although about the same distance from cluster 3, falls outside the outer boundary and therefore suggests much less about the clustering. It is intrinsically less likely that cluster 3 has a greater extent on the right side because the outer boundary derives from the entire dataset. Point D lies equidistant from clusters 1, 2, and 3 and therefore is more interesting than points A and B because the presence of several data records in this vicinity would have much greater implications for the model.

This intuitive and low-dimensional picture suggests a useful computational definition for the interestingness of a record: a record is *interesting* when it lies close to a boundary between one cluster and the rest [6]. Interestingness decreases with distance from such a boundary, but increases with proximity to multiple boundaries.

Figure 5.11 shows the same three clusters with notional boundaries drawn between them—ignore for now how these boundaries are computed. Note that these boundaries terminate at the outer boundary. Now we can ignore particular points and think in terms of regions in the space, and the interestingness of regions. The region in the center is close to three boundaries and so is maximally interesting; the regions between pairs of clusters are also interesting, more so closer to the 'middle' of the gap between them. These regions make it clear why D is a more interesting record than A.

Since the boundaries shown in the figure are derived from considering one cluster versus the rest of the data, the point D is in a region that no cluster claims—each of these boundaries indicates that point D is not in cluster 1, not in cluster 2, and not in cluster 3. This is also another reason why point D (and the region it is in) are

Fig. 5.11 Same clustering
with boundaries between each
cluster and the remaining data
(*dotted lines*)

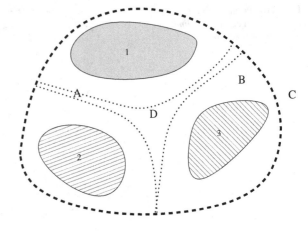

Fig. 5.12 A slight variation in
the boundaries creates regions
with different implications

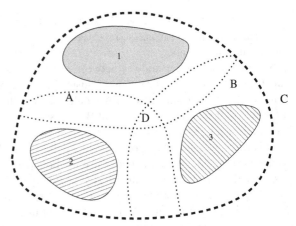

interesting—on the face of it, D's presence suggests a potential fourth cluster for
which it is the only exemplar (so far).

Another possibility is shown in Fig. 5.12. Now *every* cluster claims D as a
member—which still makes it interesting, but in a different way. Also, there is a
slightly stronger implication that point A "belongs to" cluster 2 and point B "belongs
to" cluster 3.

The advantage of thinking in terms of regions rather than points is that it now
becomes possible actively to acquire data of a particular kind. In other words, in
settings where directing the gathering of data is possible, these regions can be used
to guide the process. If there are no data to be found in these regions, then the
clustering is robust. However, if new data is gathered that falls into these regions,
the model is clearly inadequate; but the collection process gathers exactly the kind
of data that is needed to improve it.

The question then becomes: how should such boundaries be constructed. Different
algorithms will produce different boundaries although, intuitively, good algorithms

will tend to produce comparable boundaries. At first sight it might seem to be reasonable to construct these boundaries using the clustering applied on the data. For example, a distance-based clustering naturally suggests placing linear boundaries midway between cluster centroids (a Voronoi diagram); a distribution-based clustering suggests placing boundaries along equiprobable contours; and a minimal spanning tree clustering suggests placing boundaries orthogonal to midpoints of edges that are not collapsed.

Choosing this kind of construction implicitly uses the entire global dataset to define the boundary between a cluster and the rest of the data. Although this seems plausible, it means that records that are far from the cluster being considered, and therefore very dissimilar to all of its records, nevertheless play a role in defining where the boundary between this cluster and the rest of the data should be.

In practice, it seems better to make the decision about the boundary between a particular cluster and the rest of the data on a more local basis, that is considering only those parts of the rest of the data that are close or similar to the cluster under consideration. With this strategy, there are two different approaches:

- Use the boundary obtained by wrapping each particular cluster; or
- Build a boundary separating each particular cluster from all of the remaining data.

5.5.3 One-Cluster Boundaries

A one-cluster approach assumes that a boundary built using the information given by the points in that cluster is the most appropriate. Points (records) sufficiently like those in the cluster are considered on the inside; *any* other point is on the outside. The properties and structure of the data in other clusters plays no role in determining this boundary. (We implicitly make this assumption in constructing the outer boundary but there we have little choice, since there are no or very few examples of points on the other side of the boundary.)

There are multiple ways to wrap each particular cluster, which we discussed in Chap. 3, but sophisticated techniques include Auto-associative Neural Networks and 1-class Support Vector Machines. This approach is rather weak because it ignores the rest of the data when constructing the boundary for each cluster.

There is also the question of how tightly to wrap the cluster. The kind of tightness that such algorithms would normally produce would leave little empty space around the points of the cluster; but the appropriate boundary for discovering points that lie between clusters should perhaps be much looser. This kind of use of wrapping algorithms has not been investigated, and it is far from clear that a loose wrapping can be said to fit a cluster effectively.

5.5.4 One-Cluster-Against-the-Rest Boundaries

The alternative is to make use of the data on the other side of the boundary, and use a standard algorithm that builds a predictor to construct the boundary.

It is conceivable, although perhaps expensive, to construct boundaries between this cluster and every other cluster individually. If there are k clusters this generates $k * (k - 1)$ boundaries, all of which could be used as part of the model. However, the boundary between the cluster we are considering and one that is far away from it is likely to be uninformative; and furthermore, the resulting boundary may slice through a region occupied by many points. It seems counterintuitive to use such a boundary. It is more natural to consider only the boundaries between a given cluster and the entire remainder of the data. Such boundaries necessarily pass through "empty" space.

By the same logic, data points that are far from the cluster under consideration should perhaps not play much part in determining exactly where the boundary will lie. This suggests that, of the algorithms described in Chap. 3, one-versus-the-rest versions of SVM are best.

Random forests are also attractive, primarily because they are such strong predictors. However, ensemble predictors define not a single boundary, but the voted totality of a set of boundaries which reduces its explanatory power.

5.6 Summary

In the multicentric setting, the space constructed from the data is rich with structure that can be exploited.

The most obvious part of the structure is the skeleton, consisting of clusters typically of different sizes, shapes, and densities and connected by edges whose lengths indicate the similarity between clusters. This graph structure may be a tree, or something richer depending on the relative positions of the clusters and the goal of the modelling. The skeleton forms the basis for downstream analysis of the data because it provides a context for understanding each individual record, and the similarity between individual records.

The less obvious, but equally important, part of the structure is the structure imposed on the empty space by the boundaries between clusters and their interpretation as defining regions that are particular interesting.

Together these two pieces enable the entire space to be categorized in the five ways that we previewed in Chap. 1:

- Normal data, which falls within the known clusters;
- Aberrant data, which fall just outside the known clusters. Such data has no substantial implications since it is explainable as due to the finiteness of the data used to build the clustering.
- Interesting data, which falls in the regions between the known clusters. Such data is more interesting the closer it is to boundaries. This kind of data suggests that the modelling of the data is inadequate, and also suggests what kind of data should be collected to resolve ambiguities in the model.
- Novel data, which falls outside the outer boundary. Such data is interpreted as coming from some unmodelled process that is not relevant to the current model, and so does not imply that the current model needs reevaluation.

- Random data, that is so far from the outer boundary that it can be ignored. Such data often signals some problem with data collection.

These two complementary views of the structure implied by the data provides a rich basis for understanding. The space itself is derived inductively from the data; the skeleton integrates local, pairwise information into a global view of the structure implied by the entire set of data (which, in turn, provides a background against which individual points and their relationships can be reinterpreted); and the empty space model derives an understanding of regions where there is no data (but there could be) that is also revealing, and has potential to drive the search for new data in a highly leveraged way.

Chapter 6
Representation by Graphs

A geometric space has the advantage that the similarity between any pair of points is independent of the presence and placement of any other points, no matter what the particular measure of similarity might be. This is computationally attractive, which is why it has been the basis of everything discussed so far.

The global strategy using a statistical-geometry approach is to first build a space (and perhaps project it); then use a metric on that space to define local similarities; and then integrate these local similarities into clusters. In this chapter, we will consider an alternate path: first build local similarity measures between some (perhaps all) pairs of records; use these to build a graph representing the dataset; embed this graph into a statistical geometry and then cluster as before.

Graphs consist of a set of nodes with weighted edges between some of the pairs of nodes. For us, the nodes will represent records, and the weights will represent similarity. Any notion of similarity will serve: we could use the dot product between records, or the root mean sum of the squared attribute differences—but, in this latter case, we no longer interpret this as Euclidean distance since there is no space for such a distance to exist in.

This graph representation of a dataset is more abstract than a geometric representation. Before we can think about clustering in such a space, we need to extend the pairwise notion of similarity associated with edge weights to a notion of similarity between nodes that are not directly connected. In other words, we need to define the transitivity of similarity.

Here there is a substantive decision that depends on the system from which the data came. One common way to extend local to global similarity is to make the global similarity the maximum of the sum of the local similarities along paths between the two nodes under consideration. This models settings in which similarity is related to ease of infection by some disease, or flow of information, where the "shortest" route between unconnected nodes is critical.

An alternative is to make the global similarity depend not just on the most heavily weighted (that is, shortest) path between the two nodes, but also on the *number* of paths between them. This models settings in which similarity is related to influence between two records (it also represents the aggregate electrical resistance between

D. B. Skillicorn, *Understanding High-Dimensional Spaces*, SpringerBriefs in Computer Science, DOI: 10.1007/978-3-642-33398-9_6, © The Author 2012

two nodes if local similarity represents the reciprocal of resistance between two connected nodes).

6.1 Building a Graph from Records

It is possible to cluster directly in the graph that represents a dataset, but this turns out to be difficult in practice. It is more usual to embed the graph into a geometric space and then cluster in that space. In other words, the overall construction is:

- Compute the local similarities between pairs of records;
- Manipulate the resulting graph to capture the desired notion of global similarity;
- Embed this graph in a geometric space whose dimensionality is $n - 1$ for a graph with n nodes;
- Project this $n - 1$-dimensional space to one of lower dimension;
- Compute a clustering in this lower-dimensional space using one of the constructions from earlier chapters.

6.2 Local Similarities

The first step, then, is to construct the local similarities from the records of the dataset. These are used to create an *adjacency matrix*, a matrix with n rows and n columns. Whenever the i th and j th rows have non-zero similarity, this value becomes the ij th and ji th entries of the matrix. All other matrix entries are zero.

There are several different ways to construct local graph similarity from pairwise record similarity in the dataset, independent of the particular metric used. Of course, in most datasets *any* two records will have some similarity, so if these are used directly then the result will be an adjacency matrix with almost every entry non-zero.

However, it seems intuitive that very small similarities, which become edges with very low edge weights, are not important to understanding the overall structure of the matrix. Variations in such low edge weights seem even less significant. Also, from a performance point of view the downstream analysis is much more efficient if the adjacency matrix can be made sparse. This motivates the use of three different techniques that threshold the edge weights, and so make the adjacency matrix sparser. They are:

1. Consider only the neighbors of a node that lie within a given radius (in whatever metric is being used); this amounts to setting all small edge weights to zero, since low-weight edges model long edges, and also means that the edge weights retained are of roughly similar magnitudes.
2. Include edges to only the k nearest neighbors of each node; this ensures that the graph forms a single connected component, but produces edge weights of very different magnitudes. (Sometimes the k mutual nearest neighbors are used because this produces better global properties.)

3. Exponentially downweight distances in the metric so that only near neighbors remain connected, by thresholding with a function of the form $e^{-\alpha d}$ for d the distance between pairs of nodes.

There is no simple way to construct an appropriately sparse adjacency matrix by recipe—the particular system that the data describes must be taken into consideration both in choosing the technique and the appropriate threshold or number of neighbors; and unfortunately the resulting clustering is sensitive to both choices. Practically it is usually necessary to compute all of the n^2 similarities before discarding the unwanted ones. This is a serious practical limitation.

6.3 Embedding Choices

Now comes the embedding. There is a trivial embedding, simply to regard the rows of the adjacency matrix as the coordinates of the points corresponding to each record in $n - 1$-dimensional space. The problem with this embedding, despite its common use, is that it is inside-out with respect to a natural understanding of the data. A row with many large non-zero entries, understood as a graph node, describes a node that is well-connected and therefore central to the graph—yet, in the embedding, it is placed far from the origin. A row with small values, understood as a graph node, is poorly connected and therefore peripheral to the graph structure—yet, in the embedding, it is placed close to the origin. This embedding fails to capture an intuitive idea of the graph structure. Furthermore, there is no straightforward way to apply inductive projections to the data (in the style of singular value decomposition) even if the embedding is normalized to form a cloud around the origin. The nodes that should appear centrally in the cloud, those that represent common or normal records (similar to many others), are at the periphery; while the unusual nodes, those that represent anomalous records, are placed centrally.

There is one exception to this: when all that is needed is the first, or principal, eigenvector which points from the origin to the 'center' of the cloud of vertices. Projecting onto this vector provides a way to rank the vertices by their importance in the graph in a useful way, and forms the core of Google's PageRank algorithm [12].

Before an embedding that makes sense can be made, the graph has to be turned "inside out" so that well-connected nodes will embed centrally and poorly connected nodes will embed peripherally. This is done by altering the adjacency matrix to one of a number of *Laplacian matrices* [30, 40].

Given an adjacency matrix A, let D be the diagonal matrix whose entries are the sum of the edge weight associated with the edges of each node of the graph (so the sum of the rows of A). Then the (combinatorial, unnormalized) Laplacian of the graph is the matrix

$$L = D - A$$

In other words, the off-diagonal entries of L are the negations of the corresponding entries of A, while the diagonal entries are the edge weight sums for each node.

There are two normalized versions of the graph Laplacian but, for various reasons, the random-walk Laplacian has substantial advantages and should be almost always preferred in practice [36]. The random walk Laplacian, L_{rw}, is defined to be:

$$L_{rw} = I - D^{-1}A$$

where I is the identity matrix, and D^{-1} is the diagonal matrix whose diagonal contains the reciprocals of the edge weight sums for each node.

A choice of normalization is effectively a choice about the kind of embedding of the graph that we are going to do. It therefore encodes information about, for example, different scales of similarity in different regions of the implicit space. If the total edge weights of the nodes are roughly the same in the whole graph, any Laplacian embedding will give similar results. If the total edge weights differ substantially, then the choice makes a great difference to the results and should be made with more attention. Constructing the similarity matrix based on spheres of a given radius will, of course, tend to produce more uniform edge weight sums than using k-nearest neighbors.

The actual embedding is done using the same data-driven projection we saw for SVD in the record-based case. (Graph embeddings are usually expressed using eigendecompositions, but we will use SVD to avoid introducing one more method.) If we compute the decomposition

$$L_{rw} = USV'$$

then the diagonal of S contains non-increasing values. In this case, the number of zero values at the end of the diagonal indicates how many connected components are present in the graph. The embedding of each node in the graph is given by the corresponding row of U. However, the columns of U are of greatest significance in the reverse order, the most important being the one associated with the *smallest* non-zero singular value.

6.4 Using the Embedding for Clustering

Truncating the decomposition can be used, as before, to create an embedding in a small number of dimensions, but the retained columns of U must be those towards the end. For example, to create a 3-dimensional embedding, and assuming the graph consists of a single connected component, columns $n-1, n-2$ and $n-3$ of U are used as coordinates, and column $n-1$ is the most significant. Also as before, this truncation is guaranteed to be a faithful representation of the graph in the smaller number of dimensions.

A truncated version of the graph can be used in a number of ways. For example, truncating at two dimensions provides an accurate planar drawing of the graph, showing as much of its structure as possible in two dimensions. The placement of each point is such that the edge lengths are distorted as little as possible with respect to the relationship between length and dissimilarity (that is, similar points are close).

Graph embedding has been used to find local outliers, but using an embedding based on the *commute time* [31].

Ordinary geometric clustering algorithms can be applied to the embedded points, and the construction gives separations between clusters that are good cuts in the graph, that is separating regions of the graph that are poorly connected to one another, but richly connected within themselves. Ranking can also be applied in the graph [49].

6.5 Summary

In previous chapters, we began with an embedding of the data, which created pairwise similarities between pairs of records based on the geometry of the embedding. This embedding was then manipulated, for example by projection, which alters the pairwise similarities, and then by imposing longer-range similarity structure implicit in the particular clustering algorithms used. For example, a density-based clustering algorithm takes an entire neighborhood of a record into account in a limited way rather than just its pairwise similarities.

In this chapter, we begin with pairwise similarities and then carry out a direct embedding in a low-dimensional space, using not only pairwise similarities but the entire structure of the graph that they imply. This uses different kinds of global integration from the local properties. For data where medium-range similarity and/or the number of similar records at different scales is important, this produces embeddings that capture deeper structure. Once a dataset has been embedded in an appropriate space, all of the techniques described in previous chapters can be applied to understand it, to create a skeleton, and to build boundaries in empty space. With a better embedding, the results of this downstream analysis are also improved.

Chapter 7
Using Models of High-Dimensional Spaces

We have shown how to think about high-dimensional spaces as multi-centered spaces, and we have introduced the algorithmic basis for constructing a skeleton for such a space. We have also seen how to divide up a space into qualitative regions that allow outliers and small clusters to be assessed and interpreted in terms of what their impact on existing models should be.

In this chapter, we show how this modelling can be applied, and how it forms the foundations for further analysis, primarily ranking of the records.

7.1 Understanding Clusters

A cluster obviously represents some set of records that are pairwise similar to one another, but the overall similarity that corresponds to "being in this cluster" is emergent from this pairwise similarity of the records. This emergent structure depends critically on how clusters are constructed, so the algorithms used for clustering necessarily determine how clusters are interpreted.

Both distance- and distribution-based cluster construction algorithms are implicitly making the assumption that a cluster is "really" a center to which some variation has been added. In other words, a cluster has two properties: a center that somehow captures the essential reason for the existence of the cluster, and some kind of extent (diameter or probability density) that captures the amount of variation in the process that generated the center. It is this assumption that justifies, for example, the abstraction of a cluster as completely defined, for a Gaussian, by a mean and standard deviation; or, for a convex hull, by the centroid and diameter of some enclosing ellipse.

In this view, "understanding" a cluster is straightforward because these abstractions provide a simple explanation—the center is a prototype record for the members of the cluster, and the extent describes the limits to variation among these members. Although the explanation is simple, it is still powerful because it is derived by inte-

D. B. Skillicorn, *Understanding High-Dimensional Spaces*, SpringerBriefs
in Computer Science, DOI: 10.1007/978-3-642-33398-9_7, © The Author 2012

grating all of the points in the cluster into an emergent entity. In other words, the cluster is built inductively, and therefore so is the model that results.

Clustering algorithms based on density do not produce such simple explanations. This is because there is no definitive idea of a center for a cluster built in this way. The typical algorithmic approach takes a record at random from the dataset as a cluster seed, and then adds to the cluster other records that are sufficiently similar to the seed record. To get intuitively appealing clusters, this similarity must decrease in some way so that "arms" that extend from the cluster are added to it, without including points that are similar distances from the center but separated from the other points of the cluster. This style of algorithm works well, but the resulting cluster is not, in general, centered around the seed point. Recreating a nominal center for such a cluster could be done by looking for sets of points with maximally similar near neighbors, but it is far from clear that this produces a reasonable answer. For instance, how much weight, if any, should be given to "arms" extending from the central region? For the same reason, there is no straightforward way to describe the *extent* of such a cluster using just a few measures.

Matrix decomposition clustering algorithms hard-wire certain assumptions about what the distribution of points along particular axes should be. This does not necessarily even translate into clusters as such, although most matrix decompositions have a clustering interpretation. For example, Singular Value Decomposition finds directions in which the data cloud has maximal extent, leading to radial clusters, as we have seen. Independent Component Analysis (ICA) finds directions in which the distribution of data points is far from Gaussian, and so tends to find small clusters with unusual cross-sections.

All this assumes that there will be detectable clusters in the data. However, for some kinds of data the distribution of points may not produce clusters at all, or the clusters may be weak and diffuse. In other words, there is no essential reason why the similarity among records in a dataset should produce a clustering. For example, a dataset that captures tastes is likely to produce a weaker cluster structure because, although there are large groups of people with similar taste in, say, music, there is also considerable variation. This variation may blur the clusters so much that it is hard to be sure what clusters are present, and where they lie.

For any dataset, looking at the clustering with a view to understanding the "meaning" of the clusters that appear will be the first analysis step. This is not a trivial step for the reasons outlined above: clusters do not necessarily reveal their meaning, and they may sometimes be hard to identify definitively. One useful approach, when the meaning of a cluster is suspected but not definitively determined, is to insert artificial data records into the dataset with attribute values set to those of a "typical" record that should fall in that cluster. Repeating the clustering with the artificial records should place them in the suspected cluster, probably quite centrally.

In domains such as retail, for example, considerable effort is spent to understand how customers cluster, and these clusters are often identified as pseudo-customers: double-income families with no children, for example. This uses two levels of abstraction: from the records to the clusters, and then from the clusters to the cluster meanings, which are then actionable in terms of product selection, opening hours, staffing, and so on.

Online retailers can also take advantage of this kind of analysis, but with more benefit because they have access to more data. For instance, a bricks-and-mortar store can only associate multiple interactions with the same customer using clunky mechanisms such as loyalty cards, while an online retailer always knows which browsing and purchase session belongs to which customer. Therefore, online retailers can use a customer's entire purchase history to cluster and this produces more robust and more powerful clusterings.

Music and video streaming sites also have a considerable amount of information about their customers although, like other sites where information is provided by users without any cost to them, the quality of the data tends to be low. They can tell that a user has played a particular song, but any like/dislike rating that the user has given to that song turns out to be very uncertain. For example, it is known that the same user's opinions about the quality of movies changes significantly from day to day.

There is an inherent symmetry in many of these kinds of datasets. We have assumed, so far, that the clustering is of the records describing perhaps customers and their purchases. However, it is equally plausible, and useful, to cluster the *attributes* based on the customer purchases. In this alternate view, the similarity between, say, items purchased depends on the pattern of customers who purchased them. Two items are similar if they are often purchased together by similar customers. Such a clustering could be computed by transposing the data matrix and repeating any of the clustering algorithms on the new data. However, biclustering algorithms, by their nature, simultaneously cluster both records and attributes so they have the added advantage that they produce both clusterings at once.

Clusters of attributes represent attributes that have the same properties with respect to the set of records (or subsets of the records). Therefore, they describe attributes that represent, in some broad sense, the same underlying properties. (This is what underlies interpretations of the data in terms of latent or hidden factors.) Often it is not obvious in the system being studied that attributes are related in this way, so finding such relationships can help to understand the system. For example, in online sales datasets, finding a set of related attributes means finding a set of objects that are often bought or approved of by some or all customers. This knowledge can be used for up-selling, recommending another of the set to someone who purchases any one of them.

Sometimes the clusters themselves reveal unsuspected knowledge. For example, an online bookseller expects to find clusters of books in genres: romance, mystery, biography, and so on. A cluster that does not fit with their intuition about genres may suggest a new "genre" that had not previously been considered—that is, a set of books that customers implicitly consider similar by their buying or preference data, but which are not (yet) apparently so from first principles. In financial data, a cluster of attributes, particularly a bicluster associated with a small potentially fraudulent group of records, may indicate which figures are being manipulated to create the fraud, and so may provide hints about how the fraud is being done.

7.2 Structure in the Set of Clusters

The next level of analysis is to consider the *set* of clusters rather than each cluster individually. At this point, we do not yet consider the skeleton and other structures—simply the characteristics of all of the clusters as clusters. The analysis is qualitative rather than computational.

However, the skeleton can be useful, even at this level, as a way to discount some of the apparent structure: to remove outlying points, and perhaps even small outlying clusters—those lying outside the outer boundary—from consideration. The reasoning is that such points and clusters are already known to be irrelevant to understanding the dataset.

One useful property is the sizes of clusters which, by themselves, reveal a lot about the dataset. For example, some datasets may have most clusters of large but similar size, with another set of much smaller clusters, also of similar size. Some datasets may have one very large cluster and almost nothing else. Some datasets may have clusters of steadily decreasing size. A sorted histogram of cluster sizes produces a shape that is characteristic of datasets at a higher level of abstraction.

An example of how this is used is in the construction of cell-phone plans. Cell-phone providers collect data about call patterns, a dataset that can then be clustered. We expect such a dataset to contain clusters because the process of calling someone is limited by social norms that constrain the possible configurations (texting is much less socially limited which is why plans for texting tend to count only total numbers of messages rather than, say, taking into account the time of day they get sent). However, clusters will differ according to, among other things, customer demographics and existing plans (which also induce clusters by the constraints they impose on the process).

Such a clustering produces a set of clusters, some of which should match the existing plans offered by the provider. However, there are three things to be learned. First, if a cluster is skewed from the notional center that the plan implies, then many customers are finding that it doesn't fit them well, so the plan should be altered. Second, if a cluster exists at a position that does not match any existing plan, then there is a need for a new plan that will satisfy, and so retain, a group of customers. Third, if no cluster (or perhaps only a very small one) exists at a point where there *is* a plan, then the plan is not serving customer needs and should be removed. Many businesses can make this kind of comparison between what their customers actually do, and what the business assumes that they do.

Examining the clusters can also provide insight into social networks and processes. In many settings with a social basis, there is one large cluster that represents, broadly, the "normal" behavior or properties of the majority group. The remainder divides into a succession of smaller groups representing more and more splintered properties. In many countries a dataset that captured political opinions or behaviors would tend to divide into three groups, two representing the majority, typically opposed, parties, and the third representing independents; as well as a large number of small clusters representing a more diverse political spectrum of opinions.

Another major set of applications where the number and size of clusters is revealing are those where the attributes are words and the records represent documents. If content-filled words such as nouns are used, then the clusters in a clustering can be interpreted as the *topics* present in the set of documents. Topics are a useful abstraction for a large set of documents, helping to understand what the set is "about". The sizes of the clusters tell us how important each topic is. The documents do not even have to be in natural language. A dataset whose records come from methods and whose attributes are keywords and identifiers in a programming language can be clustered into "topics"; and these topics show which methods are co-maintained [21].

Another related application is *search disambiguation*. When words have multiple meanings, as they often do in natural languages, pages returned as the result of a search are a mixture of those relating to each of the meanings. Some search engines (for example, www.yippy.com) then cluster the returned pages based on their total word uses, and then present these clusters as the initial stage of the result. Users can then select which of the clusters contains the meanings, and so the pages, that they were searching for.

7.2.1 Semantic Stratified Sampling

A second major task using the results of a clustering is sampling or summarization. In its simplest form, one record can be selected from each cluster. This list of records forms a stratified sample of the dataset but, unlike ordinary stratified sampling, the choice of records is semantic. The clustering has, as usual, integrated the local information in the records into global information that can then be used to select a few records in a meaningful way—they are maximally spread across the structure in the data.

For example, if the records represent the words used in a set of documents, then the clusters represent topics. Sampling one document from each cluster provides a subset of documents that, by construction, spans the topics. At a finer grain, if the records describe the word usage of a set of sentences from a single document, then this sample is actually a reasonable summary of the document [43]. The clustering divides up the sentences so that the sentences in each cluster are quite repetitious (as they usually are in natural language), and the different clusters represent different subtopics.

This kind of semantic stratified sampling is also useful in learning. Someone who knows nothing about a particular area can easily find a list of documents relevant to the area (books or, increasingly, web pages), but it is much harder to know which ones to read, since such a list usually is very redundant. A stratified sample removes the redundancy, and provides a shorter list that still has the same coverage. (Of course, this is a very crude approach to learning—we will see more sophisticated approaches in the following sections.)

There are similar applications in open-source intelligence gathering. For example, an analyst may download all of the postings in some forum. Rather than reading through the entire set in some order, the analyst may first use this kind of clustering and stratified sampling to get a sense of typical areas of discussion and their relative importance. This *sensemaking* provides both a context and a way to focus on clusters of the greatest interest.

Of course, a number of issues remain. Rather than selecting a single record from each cluster, perhaps it would be more useful to select a fixed fraction of the records in each cluster. This produces a stratified sample that is more uniform across all of the documents. And the difficult issue remains of *which* record(s) to select from each cluster—see the discussion above about representative points.

Finally, a third application emphasizes the small outlying clusters or the points that do not fall in any of the clusters, the *outliers*. In many settings, for example network intrusion detection, it is this outlying structure that is of primary interest, and the larger, more central clusters are only of interest as a background against which to detect outliers. Most work in this area takes a single-centered view and includes all points in the analysis. Better results are obtained, in general, by assuming a multicentric view of the data and applying an outer boundary before examining outlier structure. First, the structure of normality is unlikely to be single centered in practice for realistic large datasets. Second, including points outside the outer boundary tends to include points that are present in the data because of collection or processing issues, rather than genuine anomalies.

In any case, simply counting the number of outlying points and clusters gives a qualitative feel for the scale of anomalies in the data; and therefore how sophisticated is the analysis required to understand them robustly.

In datasets that reflect normal social activities it is rare for there to be single outlying points. Social interactions tend to draw together even individuals who would otherwise appear unusual; and even the most unusual tastes tend to involve some social interaction. Therefore in datasets reflecting social processes the presence of an outlier might suggest a lone wolf. Such individuals are often of concern in intelligence and counterterrorism settings.

Examining the scale and frequency of clusters can reveal much about a dataset; but, of course, using the extra information in the skeleton is even more revealing, and we turn to this now.

7.3 Ranking Using the Skeleton

The skeleton allows us to examine the *relationships* between the clusters, including the strengths of each association based on the weight or similarity associated with the edges joining pairs of clusters.

The edges joining clusters represent a qualitatively different kind of similarity from the edges joining data records, even when they were built in analogous ways. That is because a cluster is a different kind of object from a record. A record is embedded in a particular location in a particular space; a cluster is a more abstract object that is associated with the space, but does not necessarily have a location or extent within it. For example, a Gaussian does not have an edge and, in a clustering

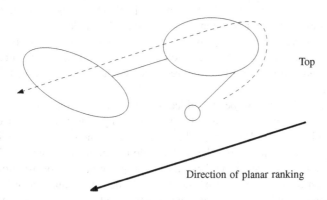

Fig. 7.1 Direct projection and skeleton-based rankings would place points from the smallest cluster differently

using a set of Gaussians, each covers the whole space (although each has a center at a location within the space). Thus there is a complex relationship between the skeleton and the space used to construct it—they are clearly related but the skeleton is, in general, an abstraction of the space.

The skeleton allows records to be ordered in ways that are not simply their positions in the statistical geometry, because it integrates the entire global information into its structure. Figure 7.1 illustrates the different outcomes of a simple ranking using the geometry and using the skeleton. A direct projection, as indicated by the solid arrow, ranks the points in the smallest cluster below most of the points in the cluster it is connected to. A skeleton-based ranking, on the other hand, ranks the points in the smallest cluster above those of both of the larger clusters.

For reasons discussed before, such rankings should only take place for points within the outer boundary, since points outside it are assumed not to arise from the same set of generative processes as the data of interest.

Where Is the Center of a Skeleton?

We have suggested that a skeleton can be of two forms: either a minimal spanning tree of the clusters, or the complete graph of the set of clusters. In both cases, there is no natural definition for the center of the skeleton. Yet the *idea* of the center of a skeleton is a compelling one—many rankings and traversals naturally use this idea.

There are three different strategies to choose the cluster that best represents the center of the data:

1. Use the structure of the weighted skeleton graph alone;
2. Use the structure of the weighted skeleton graph *and* properties of the clusters;
3. Use an embedding of the skeleton into a geometry and use the center of this geometry.

For the complete-graph skeleton, a center can be chosen using an algorithm originally developed to help locate facilities centrally [19]. This finds the node of the graph with the shortest weighted distance to all of the other nodes.

With access to the properties of the clusters, a plausible choice is the node corresponding to the largest cluster. This cluster, in many datasets, captures the most-common, and therefore most-normal records, which is often what we think of intuitively as the center.

The complete graph can also be embedded into $c - 1$-dimensional space (if there are c clusters) using the constructions of Chap. 6, that is by converting the adjacency matrix of the skeleton, regarded as a graph, to a Laplacian and using location in the space spanned by the eigenvectors. The center node is then the one that lies closest to the origin in this space. With the "inside-out" property of this construction, the node lying closest to the origin will be the one with the largest number of heavier edges connecting it to other nodes. This is a plausible candidate for the most central cluster.

For a minimal spanning tree skeleton, the central node is the one that is most naturally considered as the root of the tree. Using properties of the graph alone, this root can be the node that is the median in the tree with respect to the number of edges, or with respect to the total edge weights of the number of edges. In other words, if the root has k outgoing edges, the number of edges (or total edge weights) on each of these k edges is more balanced than for any other node.

With access to the properties of the clusters, the root could be chosen to be the largest cluster, for the same reasons as in the complete graph case; or it could be chosen to be the median of the node sizes in the tree—in other words, the node sizes associated with each outgoing edge are as balanced as they can be.

In the same way as before, the spanning tree can be embedded into $c - 1$-dimensional space, and the root taken to be the node closest to the origin in the embedding. Note that the embeddings of the complete graph and the equivalent spanning tree will not necessarily consider the same cluster to be the center.

There is no definitively best solution to which node should be the center of a skeleton. Different domains and applications may be best served by different choices—although choosing the largest cluster appears to be the most natural generic solution, and therefore should probably be the default.

Ranking from Center to Edge

The most useful rankings are derived from traversals from center to edge, and edge to center, where the "center" has been constructed as discussed in the previous section.

A traversal from the center to the edges ranks the records with the most important first, as long as most central is a reasonable surrogate for most important. For example, for a set of documents this ranking places, at the top of the list, the most central document of the most central cluster. The bottom of the ranking contains the most unusual document, which is probably not very important in many document sets.

A ranking like this is the basis for learning systems, since it defines the order in which content should be presented to a student.

A ranking in its basic form is a cumbersome basis for learning, however, because it is usually very repetitive. Documents that appear near the center are very similar. What a learner actually needs is something intuitively like a spiral through the material: starting near the center, but only reading some documents, and moving "outwards" from more central material to more peripheral material. Usually, the sampling can become more spaced since there is inherently less relevant content in the peripheral documents.

The idea of a "spiral" is natural given a skeleton, especially when the skeleton is a spanning tree, since the lateral movement associated with a spiral corresponds to moving from subtree to subtree in the spanning tree—in other words, a spiral is a top-down breadth-first traversal.

The ranking reduces the high-dimensional structure of a spiral to sampling along the continuum given by the skeleton. This sampling may, and probably should be, non-linear with the number of samples decreasing with distance from the center. The rate of sampling could also be user-dependent. For example, if the ranking is divided into contiguous segments, a user might have to pass a test to move into the next segment. Failing this might result in being shown fresh content from the current segment.

This ranking is also the basis for *divergent search*. Conventional search engines find more about concepts that the user already knows and can describe using search terms. However, it is becoming increasingly important to discover new concepts, not at random but in a way contextualized by what is already known and understood. Given a set of documents, say web pages in response to a search query, a good search engine will rank them so that the most relevant documents are at the top of the list. However, skipping the tightly packed top of the ranked list and looking at lower ranked web pages is one way to discover new concepts, still contextualized because they are relevant to the original search query [46].

Ranking from Edge to Center

Records can also be ranked from the edges to the center. Such a ranking is at the heart of most adversarial analysis, in fraud, law enforcement, counterintelligence, and counterterrorism. That is because, in these domains, it is plausible to assume that common equals innocuous. Therefore any record that is similar to many others is almost certainly not of interest. Records that do not resemble any others, or which occur in small, outlying clusters are potentially the result of adversarial activity, both inherently less typical or normal activities, and also activities related to active concealment.

A ranking from edges to center places the most suspicious records at the top. In many settings, there are not enough resources to investigate every potentially suspicious record so the ranking concentrates attention on the most suspicious. Therefore, it is important to do this ranking well.

For example, consider the tax fraud example with which we began Chap. 1. The set of all tax returns typically clusters at multiple levels: the routinely employed, the self-employed, those who live on investment income, and a number of other more specialized groups. Within each of these high-level differentiated groups there will be finer structure and therefore smaller clusters. For example, the routinely employed might form a single long cluster because the relationships between, say, income, deductions, and tax payable are highly correlated but the values have very different magnitudes. In contrast, the substructure associated with professionals and the self-employed typically forms many different clusters because the relationships between the attributes is more complex. To say it another way, there are many more rules that potentially apply to such individuals and these rules tend to induce clusters. Fraudulent tax returns differ from normal ones—but fraud moves the point corresponding to that tax return away from the point in the space where it "should" be. Because the structure of where points "should" be is so complex, it is not trivial to discover such points. They may be outliers from the cluster of similar non-tax-evading returns, but they will not be outliers in any global sense—hence the need to use all of the sophistication of the skeleton to find them.

A ranking of tax return data from edge to center will place returns that are global outliers (within the outer boundary) at the top of the list; followed by records that are local outliers (even though they may fall between existing clusters, the skeleton detects their structurally peripheral nature); and then records that appear in large clusters (and so are assumed to be honest).

Many other adversarial domains have a similar structure. Normal, that is innocuous records, tend to resemble one another in some general way, but there is considerable structure to normality. For example, in medical fraud, the number of different but legitimate procedures and procedure combinations is enormous, but the number of patients involved is large enough that even rare but normal combinations occur with some frequency in the data. In customs and border crossing applications, the number of travel patterns is large—but so is the number of travellers.

Detecting anomalies in such data by applying simple outlier detection mechanisms that are implicitly single centered finds only the outermost points—which are, in any case, likely to be points that lie outside the outer boundary—while missing points that are anomalous but interior to the global structure. Applying the multicentric approach and building the skeleton allows the very extreme points to be properly discounted, while allowing subtler but more important anomalies to be identified.

Another important application domain where ranking from edge to center is important is in *corpus analytics*, especially in intelligence applications such as open-source intelligence analysis. In such settings, analysts have access to a large set of documents, only a small fraction of which are potentially of interest. For example, many public or semi-public forums contain postings on a variety of topics, few of which are of interest to intelligence analysts—but a small minority of postings may be relevant. Generating data on word usage within each document, creating the appropriate statistical geometry, and then ranking the documents from edges to center provides a way to focus analyst attention on documents of particular interest. Documents that are simply unusual in the sense that they use words that no other document uses will be placed far from the center of the structure, and so will be ignored as outside the outer boundary. Documents that use words in ways that do not correlate strongly with the way those words are used in the majority of documents will be placed in positions that the skeleton will understand as interesting. In both cases, the model does exactly the right thing to assist an analyst to decide which documents need to be examined. As a side-effect, the model also indicates which documents can be ignored.

Another domain where the model's ability to rank documents by interest is *e-discovery*. Here lawyers are typically presented with a large set of electronic documents, perhaps emails, and want to extract from them any useful knowledge that might play a role in the legal action, preferably without having to read all of them.

Rankings from Edge to Edge

So far we have considered only rankings from center to the edges, but it also possible, and useful, to consider rankings from one edge to the opposite edge. However, what constitutes an "edge" let alone an "opposite edge" is not straightforward, and depends on how the skeleton was constructed.

An edge-to-edge traversal must pass through the center of the skeleton. If the skeleton is a spanning tree, then it is a path from the leaf selected as one edge to the lead selected as the other edge, and all of the other subtrees are omitted. This is one place where using a spanning tree as the skeleton is not very useful. If the spanning tree has been embedded in a geometry, then an edge-to-edge traversal can be implemented by a planar sweep along the line joining the two edges (leaves), ranking by order of intersection with the sweeping plane. In other words, the ranking is the projection of points onto the line joining the two edge points.

If the skeleton is a complete graph, then a graph-based edge-to-edge traversal is just the weighted breadth-first traversal from the node representing one edge to the node representing the other. Such a traversal need not be commutative, so two different rankings can be produced from the same pair of edge nodes, by building them in different orders. If the complete graph has been embedded in a geometry, an edge-to-edge traversal can be implemented by projection along the line joining the two nodes, just as for the spanning-tree case.

A powerful example of the use of edge-to-edge ranking is the detection of deception in textual data. A model of the changes that occur when deception is present has been developed empirically, by observing sets of documents that do and do not contain deception [41]—initially documents written by students, but now extensively validated over large sets of documents and authors.

The model is based on changes in the rates of use of 86 different words, in four categories: first-person singular pronouns ("I", "me"); exclusive words that signal the beginning of some refinement of content ("but", "or", "whereas"); words associated with negative emotions ("anger", "dislike"); and action verbs ("go", "lead"). When deception is present, the rates of use of first-person singular pronouns and exclusive words *decrease*, while the rates of use of negative-emotion words and action verbs *increase*.

Such a model cannot be applied to a single document in isolation because of its dependence on increases and decreases, relative to the norms of a particular document type. For example, in business writing, first-person singular pronouns are vanishingly rare, so a single one may create an entirely misleading appearance of honesty. In travel writing, action verbs are common and may create a similarly misleading appearance of deception.

However, given a *set* of documents, it is possible to rank them from most to least deceptive (still without being able to impose a definitive boundary between deceptive and non-deceptive). Given a set of n documents, a dataset matrix of size $n \times 86$ can be created, with the ijth entry giving the frequency of the jth model word in the ith document. Those words in the first-person singular pronoun and exclusive words categories need to have their magnitudes reversed so that, across the matrix, increasing magnitude is a stronger sign of deception.

Deception scores can be computed for each document by adding up the entries in each row. The higher the resulting sum, the more deceptive that document is in comparison to the rest. In the framework we have been using, each document corresponds to a point in 86-dimensional space; the greater the sum of each row, the further each point lies in the positive hyperquadrant of this space; so the ranking implied by simple addition is a projection onto the line passing through the points $(1, 1, \ldots, 1)$ and $(-1, -1, \ldots, -1)$.

While this is effective, it is possible to do better. Not all words are equally strong signals, especially in certain types of documents, but a simple sum treats them all as equivalent. Applying a singular value decomposition to the 86-dimensional space downweights the effect of dimensions (and so model words that show little variation across the dataset and/or have only small frequencies), and upweights words whose frequencies are large or variable. Projecting onto a line through $(s_1, s_2, \ldots, s_k)$ and $(-s_1, -s_2, \ldots, -s_k)$ (where the s_i are the k largest singular values), for some truncated number of dimensions k, produces a better ranking of the documents by relative deceptiveness. (In practice, authors tend to vary fairly independently on their styles with respect to first-person singular pronouns and use of exclusive words, so deception appears to be a 2- or 3-factor process.)

Including a clustering step provides an even more sophisticated understanding of the data. For example, if the documents have been written by a small group of authors, it is useful to consider whether the clusters are related to authorship or not. If each cluster is by a single author, then we conclude that each author has a characteristic style or level of deceptiveness. If there are multiple clusters by the same author, then we conclude that the author uses different levels of deception in different documents, and considering the differences may be instructive. If the clusters are not correlated with the authors at all, then deceptiveness is determined by the environment and not by the author.

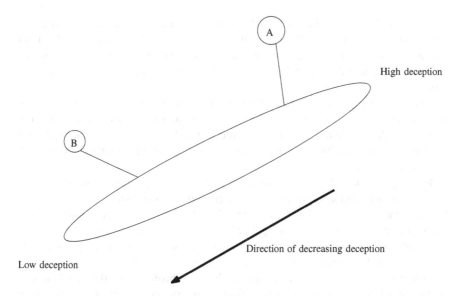

Fig. 7.2 Clusters A and B are ranked differently using the clustering

A clustering and skeleton refines the ranking based on projected deception score. For example, Fig. 7.2 shows the situation where the majority of documents form a homogeneous group oriented along an axis from high to low deceptiveness, but there are two small clusters of documents that, although they are respectively high and low in deceptiveness, are characteristically different from the main, larger group of documents.

A ranking using projection to two dimensions from the original 86-dimensional space would rank the documents in Cluster A towards, but not at, the top and the documents in Cluster B towards, but not at, the bottom of an ordering by deceptiveness. However, the information from the clustering suggests that Cluster A should perhaps rank above the main cluster and Cluster B below it; or at least they should receive more attention than their position in the initial ranking would indicate.

Another application where a ranking from edge to edge has been used is to examine a document corpus for Jihadi language. Koppel et al. [34] built a model of Jihadi word use. Taking translations of the top 100 words in this model and generating a document-word matrix using the postings in a forum and this set of words allowed the entire forum to be ranked in order of potential Jihadi content [45].

Traversal from a Point

Many algorithms are based upon the ability to find the nearest neighbor of a point, or perhaps some small set of near neighbors. Once a statistical geometry has been constructed, this idea can be improved by considering the nearest neighbors of a given point in the skeleton, that is basing similarity on *distance in the skeleton* rather than distance in the geometry. In general, this will provide better information because the skeleton encodes and integrates global information into what is, in essence, a local problem.

One major application of finding the nearest neighbor of a given point is in *recommender systems*. Such systems accumulate information about what particular users like or have done. When new users want a recommendation of things to like or do, the system looks for a similar older record (or a set of them) and recommends something from other record(s).

Finding near neighbors is an important part of making good recommendations. But there is a further complication: the older records must somehow contain more than the new one does, so that there is something fresh to recommend. Therefore the solution requires finding a near neighbor in some "direction".

In ordinary recommendation spaces making this idea of direction operational is quite difficult. One approach is to choose the direction of "more positive", that is towards records that contain fewer zeros, which is sensible if the data contain, say, ratings of movies or songs. In a statistical geometry, we are on firmer ground in defining direction—direction means "along a traversal". Although there are several different possible traversals, this reduces the difficulty of the choice and makes it more meaningful. For example, on a traversal from center to edges, an inward neighbor is more commonplace than the starting point, while an outward neighbor is more unusual. Which one is most appropriate depends on the application domain. Even within, say, a music recommendation system, a user might want different recommendations at different times. Similarly, with an edge-to-edge traversal, a near neighbor in one direction has *more* of the property involved, while one in the other direction has *less*. The presence of the skeleton makes it possible to look for the semantically nearest neighbors rather than just the geometrically nearest neighbors.

A more difficult problem in recommender systems, and one that has not yet been solved effectively, is to make recommendations that are similar but not too similar. For example, admit to buying a single book by a popular and prolific author such as Agatha Christie and your recommendation list will fill with the other 199 of her books. At one level, this is sensible—if you liked one Christie book, you might like others. But at another level it is unhelpful because you probably already know (or can easily find out) that Christie wrote many books; but you might like to be told about similar authors such as Dorothy Sayers. Getting the *amount* of similarity right is quite difficult: too much and the recommendation is weak; too little and it is too far from the starting point.

Semantic nearest neighbors can help this problem. One possible solution is to recommend not the nearest neighbor, but the nearest neighbor in an adjacent cluster. Such a neighbor is locally dissimilar, because of coming from a different cluster, but globally similar, because of being close in the skeleton.

Social networks face a similar computational problem. Systems supporting such networks often suggest "someone you might know" but these suggestions are often unhelpful because the person suggested is already too close in the social network.

The value added comes from suggesting someone the user would not have thought of unaided. Once again, someone at a small distance in the semantic space given by the skeleton is likely to be better than someone at a small geometric distance.

7.4 Ranking Using Empty Space

There is another alternative to ranking based on the skeleton, and that is to use the structure of empty space. Of course, if all records are part of the skeleton then no records appear in empty space. Rather we consider a pruned skeleton that contains only clusters of, say, size above a given threshold, and then use empty space ranking to categorize the points that do not lie in any of these clusters.

Necessarily, such rankings emphasize the extremes of the dataset, and have little to say about the common, or normal records. Nevertheless, ranking using empty space complements ranking using the skeleton precisely because it depends less on the parts of the dataset where large numbers of similar records are present, and more on those parts where records are rare or non-existent.

Our definition of the interestingness of a record is how close it is to boundaries between clusters—where the measure increases with closeness, and also with the number of boundaries involved. Intuitively, such a measure is straightforward, but a workable definition is more difficult because only boundaries that pass through the region of interest should really be taken into account. Distance from some remote boundary should not have any effect on interestingness. (This is another aspect of the issue of whether to build boundaries between all pairs of clusters or between each one and the rest.)

A plausible measure is to compute the reciprocal of the distance from a point to (the nearest point on) each boundary and then sum these over all of the boundaries. This computes appropriate values for isolated records: the measure is large for points close to a boundary and becomes larger if they are close to multiple boundaries. It includes terms derived from distant boundaries, but these are typically small since the distances in the denominators are large. As a practical tactic, it makes sense not to compute the measure for points in sufficiently large clusters. For example, one arm of a density-derived cluster might actually be quite close to the boundary between that cluster and the rest; whether such a point should be accounted interesting depends on the setting.

Points that fall outside the outer boundary will tend to appear interesting but they should not be included in the calculation for two reasons. First, as discussed before, such points are not considered an integral part of the data and so not robustly analyzable. Second, the boundaries between clusters terminate at the outer boundary, so it is not possible, without a lot more computation, to compute distances to them in a sensible way.

Using this measure, all of the points or some subset of the more isolated ones can be ranked using this measure so that the most interesting are at the top. This is most

Fig. 7.3 Clusters A and B
will be ranked in different
orders using the skeleton or
empty space interestingness

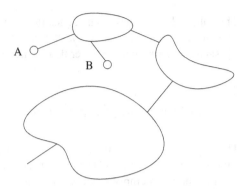

useful in adversarial settings, where (small sets of) points that do not fit well into
existing clusters are likely to be of greatest concern.

The ranking produced using interestingness and the ranking produced using the
skeleton and starting from the edges will normally agree in some general way; but
the rankings will differ especially for points that lie near several boundaries. Such
points will associate, in the skeleton, with whichever cluster they are "closest to"
(although perhaps not very close). The extra information that they have similarities
to other clusters of the same magnitude is lost or obscured by the way in which the
skeleton is constructed.

Figure 7.3 shows an example, with some clusters and part of the skeleton indicated
by the solid lines connecting the clusters. Cluster A will be ranked as more anomalous
than Cluster B because it is further away from its parent cluster in the skeleton.
Using an interestingness ranking derived from empty space, Cluster B is clearly
more interesting than Cluster A, since it lies close to multiple boundaries between
the larger clusters.

Probing for New Data

The other practical advantage of empty space is that it defines not just the interestingness of a subset of the existing data, but also that it defines the interestingness
of regions of the statistical geometry. This creates the possibility of *template-driven
data discovery*.

Given a region of the statistical geometry, it is possible to reverse engineer the
kind of data points that would fall into that region. This is not entirely straightforward because the statistical geometry is an abstraction of the dataset, for example
a projection into fewer dimensions. For a given point in the geometry, there will
typically be several data records that map to it. Depending on the particular way in
which the geometry is constructed from the data, some attributes in the data record
will have particular ranges that are all equivalent (in the sense that they all map to
the same place). This construction can also be checked by seeing whether abstracted
points do in fact map to the right place.

With such abstracted points, two applications become possible. First, often much more data has been collected than is actually used for modelling. An abstracted point can be turned into a query that can be used to interrogate this larger dataset for more data records—but not just any records; records that are particularly interesting, and therefore which have the most to reveal about the potential need to modify the model. In other words, template-driven discovery can request exactly the most useful records from any larger available dataset.

Second, even if a larger dataset is not available, template-driven data discovery can be used as an investigation tool in the real world. For example, a region that seems particularly interesting, whether or not there are any existing data points in it, can suggest trying to gather data that *would* fall into such a region. Either finding such data, or not finding it, provides extra knowledge about the system being investigated.

7.4.1 Applications to Streaming Data

A special case of the problem we have been considering is one where the focus is almost entirely on new data that is arriving in a streaming way, that is at such a high rate that it cannot be stored, except briefly. The initial model (the clustering) is built from some prefix of the data stream but its purpose is primarily its explanatory power for the data that follows. This is not a qualitatively different problem from the ones we have posed, but it is instructive to consider the benefits of using the initial data to build a skeleton and empty space model, rather than, say, a Bayesian prior.

There are four main benefits:

1. If the record falls within a cluster, then many of its higher-level or more abstract properties can be inferred from those of its cluster. For example, the size or shape of the cluster have already provided at least some information about its "meaning", and even deeper senses of its "meaning" may also have been induced from the initial data.
2. If a record falls outside a cluster, then its "meaning" can be inferred from the empty-space model. In particular, it is possible to tell whether the newly-arrived record is interesting, novel, or random. An interesting record may be highlighted to a human in the loop, for example.
3. The rate at which newly-arriving records fall outside of the existing structures provides information on whether the system from which the data comes is changing enough that models need to be rebuilt. This information can come from records that fall within clusters. For example, if many fall to one side of a cluster, then the notional center of the cluster may be changing. A number of interesting records falling in the same region suggest the emergence of a new (or previously uncaptured) cluster. A number of novel records falling in the same region suggest that the data has a greater extent than realized when the clustering was built, or that the data is changing in a global way. A number of random records falling in the same region suggest either an unmodelled data-collection issue, or a misplaced assumption that records considered as random are actually novel.

All of these indications can be used to decide if and when the clustering needs to be updated or rebuilt to reflect structure learned from newer data. The ability to decide which records are most informative about the deficiencies of the model makes it possible to store such records, so that the model update has maximally informative information available. In general, if such records are relatively rare in the data stream, the amount of storage will be of a practical size.

4. The clustering provides better approaches to sampling problems such as the Vacation Snapshot Problem [7] where the goal is to sample a stream (of images in this case) so that the sample has good coverage of the entire stream. In other words, the sample should not be repetitive, and should include examples of as many "different" records as possible. This problem has applications in, for example, UAV image capture.

   Current approaches to this problem use Bayesian surprise as the measure of when to keep the current record permanently [27]. Bayesian surprise builds priors based on the records seen so far, and selects the next record to be collected for the sample if its probability with respect to the prior is low. The prior is then updated to reflect the latest record.

   Using a clustering instead is more expensive, because of the cost of the initial clustering and because it is more expensive to update. However, it is also more effective because the level of background knowledge it provides is much more substantial than just a prior. In particular, Bayesian surprise treats all unexpected new records as equivalent, while a clustering separates them into subcategories with different meanings—only some of which suggest that such a record should be taken for the sample. In other words, random, novel or interesting records can all have high Bayesian surprise, but do not have equivalent levels of significance.

7.4.2 Concealment

In adversarial settings, people who wish to conceal themselves or their activities will try to change attribute values to seem more innocuous than they actually are. This cannot be completely successful, since there must be some property that distinguishes their adversarial activity from others. It is, of course, critical that attributes whose values are different for adversaries are collected, or else the distinction is impossible to discover. However, it is unlikely that such distinctions can be made based on the values of single attribute, or even a small set. So it is important that the technique used to build the statistical geometry does not do anything to obscure what may be small differences.

Even with a strong algorithmic approach, explicit concealment by adversaries may still cause difficulties. One way to think about the effect of concealment is that, in the statistical geometry, it moves points from where they "should be" to different locations. For example, an adversary may (try to) move the point associated with their record towards a larger cluster. In other words, one of the indicators for the presence of a small, adversarial cluster is that it looks like a fringe on a larger, innocuous cluster—

the result of the tension between the differences created by whatever unusual activities the adversarial action involves, and the attempt to seem as similar to normality as possible.

One side-effect of such manipulation of the data that may be visible is an emptiness near a boundary with an unusual number of points between it and a nearby cluster.

7.5 Summary

We have explored four ways in which the results of a clustering can be exploited to understand a high-dimensional dataset. The first is to explore the "meaning" of clusters as groupings, using what they tell us about which records belong together and trying to extract or assign a meaning to this set of records. The second is to consider the clusters as set and consider their number, sizes, and other properties. Together, these two analyses are the usual payoffs from clustering data.

However, there are much more substantial payoffs obtained from considering the higher-level structures we have proposed. The skeleton enables many kinds of rankings of the data records, both global and local. These rankings highlight the most important, interesting, or significant records with respect to a variety of objective functions. An important consequence is that, for large datasets, an analyst can focus on a (much) smaller set of records with confidence. Sampling across the entire dataset can also be improved because of the global context implicit in the clustering, enabling such sampling to acquire a semantic component.

For records that are unusual, and for newly-acquired records, the empty-space model also enables ranking—this time, by measures of how unusual such a record is in a much richer way than simply considering global or local outliers. Again, the richness comes from the detailed global context in which each such record is considered.

Chapter 8
Including Contextual Information

In all of the previous chapters, we have assumed, perhaps implicitly, that under-standing high-dimensional spaces was something that happened in isolation, and only once for each particular dataset. Nothing could be further from the truth. The process of exploring and understanding a dataset is always iterative, and the results of each round, and the deeper understanding that comes from it, inform the strategy and tactics of the next round.

In this chapter, we explore a deeper and more difficult issue: how models of a dataset are, or should be, altered to reflect the wider context in which the models are constructed and used. A model is built with a purpose; a model is built in a particular organizational context; and a model is built with a particular level of sophistication, and all of these can and will change over time. Some of the changes will take place over years; but some of them will happen over much shorter time frames as an analyst gets a new idea and wants to explore it.

8.1 What is Context?

In this chapter, we will assume that the context is everything except the models that have been built from the data: the clusterings and the derived structures, such as rankings. The context therefore includes everything else that has some effect on the models: the data, the analyst and the larger organization in which the analyst is set, and the algorithmic framework.

8.1.1 Changing Data

The most obvious way in which the context can change is that the data changes. This can happen in three important ways:

D. B. Skillicorn, *Understanding High-Dimensional Spaces*, SpringerBriefs
in Computer Science, DOI: 10.1007/978-3-642-33398-9_8, © The Author 2012

1. More data is collected. For almost all real-world datasets, there is more data to be had by waiting longer; and in many settings there is a natural need to collect new data to see whether the system it comes from is changing. All model building must be designed to update when the newly arriving data suggests that the system is changing, but few actually are.
2. More attributes are collected. In general, collecting new records with the same shape as older ones is much more common than collecting more information associated with existing records. However, if a clustering is clearly inadequate, or captures similarity structure that is different from the one required, it may be sensible to collect new attributes (and perhaps discard some old ones).
3. The importance of attributes is rebalanced. As we have discussed, any definition of similarity must commit to a relationship between variation in one attribute and variation in others. Sometimes, with deeper understanding, these relationships may be better understood, suggesting either a fresh definition of similarity or a reweighting of attributes in the current one.

Any of these changes in context caused by changes in the data have implications for the existing models and derived structures and require rebuilding models, either completely fresh from the beginning, or in an incremental way.

8.1.2 Changing Analyst and Organizational Properties

An important part of the context, and one that is harder to deal with because it is more complex and sophisticated, is the set of mental models associated with each analyst and the organization from which she comes. Context changing mental models can happen in these four ways:

1. The analyst or organization can acquire new knowledge from outside of the modelling environment. There are many potential ways in which this could happen: for example, new domain knowledge or new explanations for structures visible in the clustering.
2. The analyst or organization may change its priorities, so that different kinds of similarity or different rankings become more important.
3. The analyst may want to explore "what if" questions to test hypotheses, and so may want to create new assumptions that behave as if they were new pieces of knowledge.
4. The analyst may come to new realizations simply by introspection, and so without any change in the environment (since, as humans, we are slow and imperfect to realize the implications of knowledge we already have).

These context changes also have implications for the existing models and derived structures.

8.1.3 Changing Algorithmic Properties

The third way in which the context can change is when the underlying technology, broadly understood, changes. For example, new algorithms can be developed; new, more powerful computing platforms can be installed; and new techniques for visualization and understanding may be constructed. Changes like these create new possibilities for models and structures of greater sophistication.

8.2 Letting Context Change the Models

So if all of these different factors can change, and such changes imply some form of change in the modelling, how are such changes to be viewed and implemented? The most obvious solution would be to recompute the entire clustering in response to any change in the context. In most real-world settings, this is unrealistically expensive. But it might not even be a good idea if it is possible. When the context changes and a new model is computed, it is often critical to understand the relationship between the previous model and the current one. It is too simplistic to throw away any understanding derived from the previous model and begin again afresh to understand the newer one. Rather what analysts need is to be able to understand how "the model" has *changed* from its older instantiation to its newer one. With this constraint, incremental model reconstruction or enhancement is more useful than complete model destruction and rebuilding. The effect of contextual changes on models, therefore, is to use them to modify existing models and structures, rather than replacing them.

Especially in the context of exploring hypotheticals, it is also critically important to be able to roll back models to a previous state, so that the effect of a hypothesis that turned out to be unhelpful can be removed from the model(s).

There are three levels of incremental modification that can be made to reflect changing context:

- Leave the underlying model(s) unchanged but alter the "view" that the analyst sees to reflect the context change;
- Leave the clustering unchanged but recompute the derived structures such as rankings to reflect the context change;
- Recompute the clustering to reflect the context change.

We now explore each of these in more detail.

8.2.1 Recomputing the View

The first way, then, to incorporate changes in context is to leave the underlying clustering and any derived models alone, but to alter the view of them presented to the analyst in a way that reflects the changed context. Obviously, this handles changes in the analyst or organization and, in a weak way, changes in the data.

For example, if an analyst indicates that a particular part of the clustering is already understood, or is of lesser importance, then the rendering of the clustering, skeleton, or empty-space boundaries can be altered to "pay more attention" to the other parts of the structures. This might mean changing the amount of screen real-estate spent on each part, for example by using a fish-eye presentation.

Another possible variation is to allow analyst-provided knowledge to alter the overlays on the clustering. There are often attributes for each record that are not, strictly speaking, an integral part of the data, but their relationships to the clustering are still of interest; for example, time of collection, geographical location, and so on. Including these attributes in the clustering tends to induce structure based on what are obtrusive but perhaps not significant properties; for example, forcing clusters based on time and geography rather than deeper structure. Nevertheless, there is often something to be learned by overlaying coding for these attributes over the clustering or derived structures.

A particular example of this is to include new data in an existing clustering. The clustering is built from data up to a certain point in time, perhaps yesterday. Newer data could be used to rebuild the entire clustering; even if this is so, it is often still useful to display the new data in the context of the previous data—that is, to embed it within the existing model without changing that model. Such a display can indicate the way in which the data is changing with time (or not); and, as we have discussed at length, the locations of new data within the current structure reveal aspects both of the structure and of the new data. This is a relatively straightforward functionality to implement, since it does not require rebuilding any models, but it remains rare in commercial data-analysis tools.

8.2.2 Recomputing Derived Structures

A second, more difficult, strategy is to keep the clustering static, but recompute the derived structures on the basis of the changed context. This provides more power than simply rendering the existing structures in a different way, but still maintains the underlying clustering unchanged.

Some of the changes that an analyst might want to cause are: ranking from different edges of the clustering; changing the density of selection along a ranking; or cutting off (truncating) one or both ends of the ranking.

For example, seeing a ranking might be enough for an analyst to decide that some of the extreme records are "really" novel rather than interesting—something that might only be detectable by examining a few of them individually. The ranking with these extremal records removed will then be more useful.

Newly arrived records can also be included in existing rankings. The positions they occupy, or their distribution along the ranked list of records provides a new level of understanding of how the data is changing over time. New forms of ranking algorithms, or variants of existing algorithms with different parameters, can also be applied at this level. Because the underlying clustering is not changed, it is straight-forward to roll back any changes in the derived structures.

8.2.3 Recomputing the Clustering

The most difficult and expensive way to include new contextual information is to change the clustering itself. There are three different ways to do this, corresponding to the three different areas in which a contextual change can have occurred.

First, a clustering can be rebuilt with a new dataset, usually a larger version of the dataset used previously. In previous steps, we considered adding new records to an existing structure, where they can be sensibly placed, and where their new positions provide information about their meaning. Now we consider aggregating them with previous records and treating them all on an equal footing—so that the emergent structure depends on the entire set of data. This might result in the newer points being placed in different places than they were in the incremental version. For example, the newer points might affect the direction of projection from the original space to a lower-dimensional one, and so change the entire setting in which the clustering is computed—something that cannot happen if the space is already determined and they are being inserted into it. Other, more substantial, forms of new data such as adding new attributes or reweighting the existing attributes can also be taken into account when a completely fresh clustering is being built.

Second, analysts may rebuild a clustering afresh to reflect new external knowledge or new goals. For example, one important way in which analyst knowledge can play a role in clustering is to add information about a few pairs of records whose local similarity is to be considered much stronger or much weaker than it would appear from the data values they contain. This is known as *semi-supervised clustering* [50]. Essentially, an analyst is providing information compelling, or hinting, that a pair of records *must* be in the same cluster, or *cannot be* in the same cluster. A very small number of such extra pieces of information can have a large effect on the resulting clustering.

Another way in which analyst knowledge can change the clustering is by reweight-ing the importance of particular records, either positively or negatively; in the limit, this can have the effect of removing some records from consideration completely.

Third, new algorithms or new algorithmic parameters can be used to carry out the clustering itself.

The problem with recomputing the clustering is that it is usually expensive—both to compute the actual clustering, and because of the need to keep around multiple models created with different contexts.

8.3 Summary

Much of the research, and many of the tools, are biased towards clustering as a one-time activity. This is typically not the case for two reasons. First, an analyst usually has to repeat clustering with different data, algorithm, and parameter choices as her understanding grows. Second, the system being modelled is seldom stable and so there is new data that either has to be understood with respect to the current model, used to alter the model, or both.

The knowledge, broadly understood, that an analyst and organization want to get from a clustering also changes over time—both as the mission changes, but also on much shorter timescales as analysts ask "what if" questions.

All of these factors mean that clusterings do not exist in isolation, but rather in families or related clusterings. Seldom can one member of the family be completely understood in isolation from the others, and comparing them, or perhaps their view of particular records, is a commonly desired activity.

Existing tools do not make it easy to take this view of clusterings. Partly this is because it is difficult to decide how to implement the contextual knowledge that comes from analyst, data, and computational environment. We have suggested a three-part taxonomy of changes: changes in the view, changes in the downstream analysis, and changes in the clusterings themselves.

Chapter 9
Conclusions

Clustering is the process of understanding the structure implicit in a dataset, as a way of understanding more deeply the system that the data describes. This is an inherently messy process, because of the ambiguity of what is meant by "understanding". It is also a complex process, because of the properties of significant real-world systems, and so the properties of the data about them.

First, real-world datasets are large in terms of the number of records that they contain. This means that any analysis is expensive: understanding the relationships among elements almost inevitably means comparing each element to most of the others. Although there are exceptions, this usually means algorithms whose running time is quadratic in the number of records.

Second, real-world datasets are wide, that is they have many attributes (although often any particular record has meaningful values for only a handful of these). Although these attributes are seldom completely independent, that is they reflect different instantiations of the same underlying or implicit processes or factors, an analyst does not usually know enough at the beginning of the analysis to determine what the dependent structure actually is. It sometimes happens that the structure within a dataset is a low-dimensional manifold within an apparently high-dimensional space, but it is more common for the data either to occupy many of the apparent dimensions, or to be made up of a collection of lower-dimensional submanifolds that are oriented in ways that partially occupy many of the dimensions. The natural embedding of such a dataset is into the space spanned by the attributes, which will therefore be a high-dimensional space.

Third, the similarity structures associated with meaningful clusters are usually far from obvious. There is a temptation to assume that clusters are roughly convex, and uniformly dense, but in most practical settings this is far from accurate.

Clustering is not really a process of finding a structure that is already "there" in the data so much as exploring a variety of possible models of the data, and deciding which one(s) are both faithful and useful. Unsurprisingly then, clustering is an iterative process resembling a conversation between analyst and modelling algorithms.

D. B. Skillicorn, *Understanding High-Dimensional Spaces*, SpringerBriefs
in Computer Science, DOI: 10.1007/978-3-642-33398-9_9, © The Author 2012

Practical clustering, at present, uses a relatively small set of standard algorithms to produce a set of clusters from data. The meaning of these clusters is then usually extracted using analyst skills.

In the academic world, there is considerable interest in algorithms that discover non-conventional clusters: clusters that have shapes far from convex, and that are intertwined in complex ways. Real-world datasets do not conform well to the implicit assumptions behind both of these. Any clustering algorithm assumes fairly straight-forward properties about what clusters are like, which often do not match with their actual properties. Academic research assumes that clusters, although they may be unusual, are few and well-separated. In fact, individual clusters are complicated in shape and properties, and it is difficult to decide definitively how many clusters are present in a dataset, and whether any particular point belongs to one cluster or another.

We have suggested that these problems can be addressed by raising the level of abstraction from clusterings as simply sets of clusters to clusterings as global structures derived from a dataset.

First, we argue that it is critical to face up to the multicentric nature of real data, particularly in contexts where it is the outliers that are of primary interest. The idea that a dataset as a whole has some kind of center is problematic in many ways— we eventually are able to define a meaningful center, but not without much deeper analysis than most clustering algorithms do.

Second, we argue that clusters should not be considered as isolated sets of internally-related points, but should be combined into a global structure, the *skeleton*, that displays the relationships of clusters to one another. The main payoff from doing so is that it enables downstream analysis of the entire dataset, primarily rankings of various kinds.

Third, we argue that there is a structure to the empty space "between" clusters. One aspect of this is the boundary between that part of the space that is inhabited by data and that part that is not (or is only very sparsely inhabited). This is important because even a large dataset cannot really fill a high-dimensional space, but it helps to understand the part that is filled. A second aspect is that the regions between the clusters have a meaning that can be used to interpret those few points that may lie in them, to interpret newly arriving points that fall in them, and to guide the acquisition of new data whose potential absence the empty spaces may suggest.

We have suggested two processes for getting from a dataset to this multifaceted understanding of its clustered structure. The first process is this:

- Embed the records as points in the natural space spanned by the attributes;
- Project this space to one of lower dimension inductively, so that both the dimensionality and the orientation of the axes is determined from the data;
- Execute a clustering algorithm in this lower-dimensional space;
- Connect the clusters into either a complete graph or a minimal spanning tree using an inter-cluster similarity measure defined for the space, and choose its center;

- Build one-versus-the-rest decision boundaries for each (major) cluster, and use these to characterize unclustered points and regions by interestingness, based on closeness to boundaries.

The second process reverses the similarity and embedding steps:

- Map each record to a node in a graph, compute pairwise similarities between records (for example, using pairwise dot product) and interpret these as edge weights;
- Convert the resulting adjacency matrix to a Laplacian matrix, and execute a singular value decomposition (or other eigendecomposition) on the matrix;
- Embed the nodes of the graph as points in the space spanned by the eigenvectors, truncating to lower dimensions as desired;
- Continue with the remaining steps just as before.

There are several benefits to this more sophisticated view of clustering. First, the level of understanding of the global relationships among the data records is much deeper. Clustering always uses pieces of local information to make explicit the global information implicit in them. The approach we have been advocating increases the power of this idea by pushing it further—extracting more global information explicitly. In turn, this enables rankings that are truly aware of the global context.

Second, this approach clarifies the somewhat muddled area of outlier detection in two ways. The relationship of an outlying point to the rest of the data is made clearer, from one perspective, by its place in the skeleton. Ranking allows outliers to be compared to one another by their "outlyingness" which is often key to deciding how to treat them, especially when resources are limited. Also the use of empty space enables a meaning to be given to regions of the space that are sparsely or totally unoccupied. For isolated points, this global view may be more meaningful than discovering the "best" way to connect each point to all of the others. Empty space with semantics also enables active searching for potentially significant data.

References

1. Achlioptas, D.: Database-friendly random projections. In: 20th ACM Symposium on Principles of Database Systems, pp. 274–281 (2001)
2. Aggarwal, C., Yu, P.: Outlier detection for high dimensional data. In: Proceedings of the 2001 ACM SIGMOD International Conference on Management of Data, pp. 37–46 (2001)
3. Bach, F., Jordan, M.: Finding clusters in independent component analysis. Technical report, UCB/CSD-02-1209, Computer Science Division, University of California, Berkeley (2002)
4. Bishop, C.: Neural Networks for Pattern Recognition. Oxford University Press, Oxford (1995)
5. Blei, D., Ng, A.Y., Jordan, M.I., Lafferty, J.: Latent dirichlet allocation. J. Mach. Learn. Res. **3**, 601–608 (2003)
6. Bourassa, M.: Interestingness: guiding the search for significant information. Ph.D. Thesis, Royal Military College of Canada (2011)
7. Bourque, E., Dudek, G.: Automated image-based mapping. In: IEEE Computer Vision and Pattern Recognition (CVPR) Workshop on Perception of Mobile Agents, pp. 61–70 (1998)
8. Breiman, L.: Random forests-random features. Technical report 567, Department of Statistics, University of California, Berkeley (1999)
9. Breiman, L.: Random forests. Mach. Learn. **45**(1), 5–32 (2001)
10. Breiman, L., Friedman, J., Olshen, R., Stone, C.: Classification and Regression Trees. Chapman and Hall, New York (1984)
11. Breunig, M., Kriegel, H.P., Ng, R., Sander, J.: LOF: Identifying density-based local outliers. In: Proceedings of ACM SIGMOD International Conference on Management of Data, pp. 93–104 (2000)
12. Bryan, K., Leise, T.: The $ 25,000,000,000 eigenvector: the linear algebra behind Google. SIAM Rev. **48**(3), 569–581 (2006)
13. Burges, C.: A tutorial on support vector machines for pattern recognition. Data Min. Knowl. Discov. **2**, 121–167 (1998)
14. Cohen, D., Skillicorn, D., Gatehouse, S., Dalrymple, I.: Signature detection in geochemical data using singular value decomposition and semi-discrete decomposition. In: 21st International Geochemical Exploration Symposium (IGES). Dublin (2003)
15. Cristianini, N., Shawe-Taylor, J.: An Introduction to Support Vector Machines and Other Kernel-Based Learning Methods. Cambridge University Press, Cambridge (2000)
16. de Vries, T., Chawla, S., Houle, M.: Finding local anomalies in very high dimensional space. In: IEEE International Conference on Data Mining, pp. 128–137 (2010)
17. Dempster, A., Laird, N., Rubin, D.: Maximum likelihood from incomplete data via the EM algorithm. J. Roy. Stat. Soc. Ser. B **39**, 138 (1977)

D. B. Skillicorn, *Understanding High-Dimensional Spaces*, SpringerBriefs
in Computer Science, DOI: 10.1007/978-3-642-33398-9, © The Author 2012

18. Draper, B., Elliott, D., Hayes, J., Baek, K.: EM in high-dimensional spaces. IEEE Trans. Syst. Man Cybern. **35**(3), 571–577 (2005)
19. Ester, M., Kriegel, H.P., Sander, J., Xu, X.: A density-based algorithm for discovering clusters in large spatial databases with noise. In: 2nd International Conference on Knowledge Discovery and Data Mining (KDD'96). AAAI Press, Portland, Oregon (1996)
20. Goldman, A.J.: Optimal center location in simple networks. Transp. Sci. **5**(2), 212–221 (1971)
21. Golub, G., van Loan, C.: Matrix Computations, 3rd edn. Johns Hopkins University Press, Baltimore (1996)
22. Grant, S., Cordy, J., Skillicorn, D.: Reverse engineering co-maintenance relationships using conceptual analysis of source code. In: Proceedings of the WCRE2011, 18th Working Conference on Reverse Engineering (2011)
23. Hubert, L., Meulman, J., Heiser, W.: Two purposes for matrix factorization: a historical appraisal. SIAM Rev. **42**(1), 68–82 (2000)
24. Hyvärinen, A.: Survey on independent component analysis. Neural Comput. Surv. **2**, 94–128 (1999)
25. Hyvärinen, A., Karhunen, J., Oja, E.: Independent Component Analysis. Wiley, New York (2001)
26. Hyvärinen, A., Oja, E.: Independent component analysis: algorithms and applications. Neural Netw. **13**(4–5), 411–430 (2000)
27. Inselberg, A., Dimsdale, B.: Parallel coordinates: a tool for visualizing multi-dimensional geometry. In: IEEE Visualization, pp. 361–378 (1990)
28. Itti, L., Baldi, P.: Bayesian surprise attracts human attention. Vis. Res. **49**(10), 1295–1306 (2009)
29. Johnson, S.: Hierarchical clustering schemes. Psychometrika **2**, 241–254 (1967)
30. Kalman, D.: A singularly valuable decomposition: the SVD of a matrix. Coll. Math. J. **27**(1), 2–23 (1996)
31. Kannan, R., Vempala, S., Vetta, A.: On clusterings: good, bad and spectral. In: Proceedings of the 41st Foundations of Computer Science (FOCS '00), p. 367 (2000)
32. Khoa, N., Chawla, S.: Robust outlier detection using commute time and eigenspace embedding. In: PAKDD, pp. 422–434 (2010)
33. Kolda, G., O'Leary, D.: A semi-discrete matrix decomposition for latent semantic indexing in information retrieval. ACM Trans. Inf. Syst. **16**, 322–346 (1998)
34. Kolda, T., O'Leary, D.: Computation and uses of the semidiscrete matrix decomposition. ACM Trans. Inf. Process. (1999)
35. Koppel, M., Akiva, N., Alshech, E., Bar, K.: Automatically classifying documents by ideological and organizational affiliation. In: Proceedings of the IEEE International Conference on Intelligence and Security Informatics (ISI 2009), pp. 176–178 (2009)
36. Kriegel, H.P., Kröger, P., Zimek, A.: Clustering high-dimensional data: A survey based on subspace clustering, pattern-based clustering, and correlation clustering. ACM Trans. Knowl. Discov. Data **3**(1), (2009)
37. von Luxburg, U.: A tutorial on spectral clustering. Technical report, 149. Max Planck Institute for Biological Cybernetics (2006)
38. MacQueen, J.: Some methods for classification and analysis of multivariate observations. In: Proceedings of 5th Berkeley Symposium on Mathematical Statistics and Probability, vol. 1, pp. 281–297. University of California Press, Berkeley (1967)
39. March, W., Ram, P., Gray, A.: Fast Euclidean minimum spanning tree: algorithm, analysis, and applications. In: Proceedings of the 16th ACM SIGKDD International Conference on Knowledge Discovery and Data Mining (2010)
40. McConnell, S., Skillicorn, D.: Semidiscrete decomposition: a bump hunting technique. In: Australasian Data Mining Workshop, pp. 75–82 (2002)

41. Mohar, B.: The Laplacian spectrum of graphs. In: Alavi, Y., Chartrand, G., Oellerman, O., Schwenk, A. (eds.) Graph Theory, Combinatorics and Applications, vol. 2, pp. 871–898. Wiley, New York (1991)
42. Newman, M., Pennebaker, J., Berry, D., Richards, J.: Lying words: predicting deception from linguistic style. Pers. Soc. Psychol. Bull. **29**, 665–675 (2003)
43. Pietronero, L., Tosattib, E., Tosattib, V., Vespignani, A.: Explaining the uneven distribution of numbers in nature: the laws of Benford and Zipf. Physica A: Stat. Mech. its Appl. **1–2**, 297–304 (2001)
44. Provost, J.: Improved document summarization and tag clouds via singular value decomposition. Master's thesis, Queen's University (2008)
45. Quinlan, J.: Induction of decision trees. Mach. Learn. **1**, 81–106 (1986)
46. Skillicorn, D.: Applying interestingness measures to Ansar forum texts. In: Proceedings of KDD 2010, Workshop on Intelligence and Security Informatics, pp. 1–9 (2010)
47. Skillicorn, D., Vats, N.: Novel information discovery for intelligence and counterterrorism. Decis. Support Syst. **43**, 1375–1382 (2006)
48. Tax, D.: One class classification. Ph.D. Thesis, Technical University Delft (2000)
49. Zhou, D., Weston, J., Gretton, A., Bousquet, O., Schölkopf, B.: Ranking on data manifolds. In: Advances in Neural Information Processing Systems 16. MIT Press, Cambridge (2004)
50. Zhu, X., Goldberg, A.: Introduction to Semi-Supervised Learning. Morgan & Claypool, San Rafael (2009)

Index

1-Class Support Vector Machines, 32

A
Aberrant records, 7
Adjacency matrix, 68
Attributes, 2, 75
Autoassociative neural network, 33

B
Bayesian surprise, 90
Biclusters, 15
  similarity, 57

C
Cell phone plans, 76
Class labels, 50
Cluster
  criteria, 48
  extent, 74
Cluster discovery, 51
Clusters, 4
  of attributes, 75
  understanding, 73
Commute time, 71
Context, 10
Convex hull, 32
Corpus analytics, 82
Cosine similarity, 17
Covers, 34

D
Deception, 83
Decision tree, 35

Density, 40
Density-based
  clustering, 23
Direction, 17
Dissimilarity, 14
Distance, 17, 39
Divergent search, 81
Document analysis, 77

E
E-discovery, 83
Embedding a graph, 69
Empty space model, 36
Euclidean distance, 13
Expectation-maximization, 26

G
Global similarity, 67
Graphs, 67

H
Hierarchical clustering, 29
  examples, 53

I
Independent component
  analysis, 24
Inductive data analysis, 3
Inductive modelling, 3
Interesting record
  definition, 61
Interesting records, 7
Internet sessions, 49

D. B. Skillicorn, *Understanding High-Dimensional Spaces*, SpringerBriefs
in Computer Science, DOI: 10.1007/978-3-642-33398-9, © The Author 2012

J
Jihadi language, 85

K
K-means, 25
    example, 52

L
Laplacian matrix, 69
Latent Dirichlet allocation, 25
Latent factors, 21
Learning, 77
Local outlier score
    example, 48
Local outliers, 8, 71
Local similarity
    graphs, 68

M
Mental models, 94
Minimum enclosing ellipse, 32
Minimum spanning tree, 29
    example, 56
Model, 8

N
Network intrusion detection, 78
Normalization, 14
Normal records, 7
Novel records, 8

O
One-class support vector machine, 32
Outer boundary, 45
Outlier detection, 5, 39
Outliers, 8, 78

P
Parallel coordinates, 24
    example, 51
Pattern-based modelling, 3
Projection, 20

R
Random forests, 35
Random projection, 22, 42
Random records, 7
Ranking, 9
Recommender systems, 86
Record data, 2
Regions, 61, 62

S
Search disambiguation, 77
Semidiscrete decomposition, 27
    example, 52
Semi-supervised clustering, 97
Sensemaking, 78
Similarity, 1
Singular value decomposition, 20, 42
    example, 48
Skeleton, 5, 30
    center, 79
Social networks, 76
State of the Union speeches, 42
Statistical geometry, 8
Streaming data, 89
Summarization, 77
Support vector machine, 35

T
Template-driven discovery, 89
Topics, 77

V
Vacation snapshot problem, 90

W
Wrapping a cluster, 31

Z
Z-scores, 14